BTEC FIRST SPORT

> Certificate
> Diploma

TEACHER SUPPORT PACK

John Honeybourne

Text © Jon Sutherland 2005
Original illustrations © Nelson Thornes Ltd 2005

The right of Jon Sutherland to be identified as author of this work has been asserted by him in accordance with the Copyright, Designs and Patents Act 1988.

All rights reserved. The copyright holders authorise ONLY users of *BTEC First Sport Tutor Support Pack* to make photocopies of the *Case Studies* and *Worksheets* for their own or their students' immediate use within the teaching context. No other rights are granted without permission in writing from the publishers or under licence from the Copyright Licensing Agency Limited. Further details of such licences (for reprographic reproduction) may be obtained from the Copyright Licensing Agency Limited, of 90 Tottenham Court Road, London W1T 4LP.

Copy by any other means or for any other purpose is strictly prohibited without prior written consent from the copyright holders. Application for such permission should be addressed to the publishers.

Any person who commits any unauthorised act in relation to this publication may be liable to criminal prosecution and civil claims for damages.

Published in 2005 by:
Nelson Thornes Ltd
Delta Place
27 Bath Road
CHELTENHAM
GL53 7TH
United Kingdom

05 06 07 08 09 / 10 9 8 7 6 5 4 3 2 1

A catalogue record for this book is available from the British Library

ISBN 0 7487 8552 3

Illustrations by Oxford Designers and Illustrators and Peters & Zabransky Ltd
Page make-up by Florence Production Ltd
Printed in Great Britain by Antony Rowe

Acknowledgements

Footballer image on Worksheet 11 illustrated by Gary Chalk © copyright Gary Chalk and Jon Sutherland.

Health and Safety signs on Worksheet 27 copyright © Instant Art (NT).

Contents

Introduction

Chapter 1	**The sports industry**	**1**
	Overview 1	
	Advice and guidance to students 1	
	Suggested lesson plan 2	
	Answers to Progress Check 2	
	Case Studies and Worksheets 5	
	IVA revision and preparation 26	
	Answers and guidelines 26	
Chapter 2	**Health, safety and injury**	**31**
	Overview 31	
	Advice and guidance to students 31	
	Suggested lesson plan 32	
	Answers to Progress Check 32	
	Case Studies and Worksheets 34	
	IVA revision and preparation 55	
	Answers and guidelines 55	
Chapter 3	**Preparation for sport**	**60**
	Overview 60	
	Advice and guidance to students 60	
	Suggested lesson plan 61	
	Answers to Progress Check 61	
	Case Studies and Worksheets 63	
	IVA revision and preparation 82	
	Answers and guidelines 82	
Chapter 4	**The body in sport**	**88**
	Overview 88	
	Advice and guidance to students 88	
	Suggested lesson plan 89	
	Answers to Progress Check 89	
	Case Studies and Worksheets 91	
	IVA revision and preparation 114	
	Answers and guidelines 114	
Chapter 5	**Sports leadership skills**	**121**
	Overview 121	
	Advice and guidance to students 121	
	Suggested lesson plan 122	
	Answers to Progress Check 122	
	Case Studies and Worksheets 124	
	IVA revision and preparation 142	
	Answers and guidelines 142

Chapter 6	**The sports performer**	**145**
	Overview 145	
	Advice and guidance to students 145	
	Suggested lesson plan 146	
	Answers to Progress Check 146	
	Case Studies and Worksheets 148	
	IVA revision and preparation 158	
	Answers and guidelines 158	
Chapter 7	**Work-based project**	**161**
	Answers and guidelines 161	

Introduction

In this support pack you will find detailed information to back up the *BTEC First Sport* students' textbook.

The BTEC First Sport course requires students to study all three of the mandatory units and three of the five available specialist units.

The first core unit, The Sports Industry, is assessed via an Integrated Vocational Assignment (IVA). Edexcel sets this and the centre, using criterion-referenced marking schemes, marks it. It is then remarked by Edexcel appointed markers.

The remaining two core units (Health, safety and injury and Preparation for sport) are assessed via internally set assignments, which aim to cover all of the criteria of the unit. This pattern is repeated for the five specialist units.

The purpose of this tutor support pack is to provide the following:

- A suggested lesson plan, based on the assumption of a 60-hour delivery schedule per unit studied.
- A series of individual and group work tasks to help underpin the understanding of the scope of the unit.
- Suggestions for IVAs, revision and assignment vehicles for each unit.

In order to assist the delivery of the units, all group and individual work tasks included in this pack have suggested guidance and answers as and when appropriate. The individual and group work tasks are further designed to encourage students to collect and generate evidence that they can use in their assignments.

CHAPTER 1: The sports industry

The information on this page is intended to help you plan and deliver your lessons using BTEC First Sport *by John Honeybourne.*

OVERVIEW

This is a key chapter intended to introduce the students to sport in general. It looks at the organisation of sport and how it features as an important part of our society.

As the knowledge content of this chapter is so important, it can be seen as a primer for all of the other chapters in the programme. There are considerable links to all other chapters. The primary goals of the chapter are:

- To look at the nature of sport, sports participation and development.
- To show how sport is organised (in the public, private and voluntary sectors).
- To show how sport is funded.
- To consider the key influences on sport, including the media.

ADVICE AND GUIDANCE TO STUDENTS

This is the only externally set and marked unit of the course. It is necessary to have a thorough understanding of the unit in terms of its content. In order to understand the demands of the IVA, it is useful to appreciate exactly what the examiners are looking for. Details are given in the following table.

PASS	To obtain a MERIT do this as well	To obtain a DISTINCTION do this as well
Define sport and sport activities locally and nationally.	Compare different sporting activities.	Evaluate the range of activity and recommend changes or improvements.
Describe how sport is organised in the private, public and voluntary sectors.	Compare how sport is organised in each sector.	Analyse each sector and prioritise future needs and development.
Identify main reasons for participation and non-participation.	Explain the main reasons.	Analyse the main reasons and offer suggestions for improvement.
Describe the main source of funding for sport.	Discuss how the main sources of funding affect sport and compare different types of funding.	Critically analyse the different sources of funding.
Identify the effect of the mass media on two different sports.	Compare the effect on two contrasting sports.	Critically evaluate the effect of the media and look at trends and influences, then draw conclusions.

CHAPTER 1 – The sports industry

SUGGESTED LESSON PLAN

TOPIC	HOURS	ACTIVITY TO USE	PAGE
Sports, sports participation and sports development Key definitions	7	Case Study 1.1 New Dutch club for David Lloyd Leisure	5
		Case Study 1.2 Growth of health clubs in Scotland	7
Participation	5	Case Study 1.3 Sport for all in East Kilbride	8
Sports development	5	Case Study 1.4 Youth development officers	9
Organisation of sport	2	Case Study 1.5 Governing bodies of sport	10
Public sector	3	Case Study 1.6 Support Local Sport Initiative	11
Private sector	3	Case Study 1.7 Personal training advertisement	12
		Case Study 1.8 New year's resolutions	13
Voluntary sector	3	Case Study 1.9 Lincolnshire Voluntary Sports Forum	14
Other agencies	3	Case Study 1.10 Tynedale's sport and recreation strategy	15
Sources of funding Funding	5	Case Study 1.11 Shooters braced for funding fight	16
		Case Study 1.12 TV funding	17
Sponsorship	4	Case Study 1.13 Sponsorship for The Owls	18
		Case Study 1.14 Funding problem for Britain's sailors	19
		Case Study 1.15 Swansea sponsorship deal	20
Key issues and the influence of the media Issues	7	Case Study 1.16 Racism on the pitch	21
		Case Study 1.17 Adrian Mutu	22
		Case Study 1.18 Real Madrid fine	23
Influence of the mass media	6	Case Study 1.19 Beckham at Real Madrid	24
		Case Study 1.20 Carling Cup violence	25
IVA revision and preparation	7		26

ANSWERS TO PROGRESS CHECK (PAGE 24, BTEC FIRST SPORT)

1 What are the main differences between sport and recreation? Give examples.

Answer
Sport involves competition between individuals or teams that is organised and includes physical activity. Recreation is a term given for an active aspect of leisure.

2 Give examples of amateur and professional sports.

Answer
An example of an amateur player is a netball player who plays for her local club or a rugby player who plays for his local club. An example of a professional is a county cricket player or a football player who plays in the Nationwide League.

3 Why are sports like badminton and golf called 'lifetime sports'?

Answer
Lifetime sports such as badminton and golf can be enjoyed throughout our lives. Just because you are older it does not mean you cannot be involved in such sports.

4 Give some of the possible reasons for people participating in the London Marathon.

Answer
The London Marathon is an event that is undertaken by seriously competitive runners, those who are looking for a personal challenge and those who are running to make money for charity.

5 Give examples of sports provision in the public, private and voluntary sectors.

Answer
Public facilities include the local leisure centre, run by the local authority and funded by the taxpayer. Private facilities include local private

CHAPTER 1 – The sports industry

health and fitness clubs. Voluntary sector facilities include the local athletics club where people can train to keep fit.

6   Describe the activities of one of the following organisations:

UEFA, Youth Sport Trust, Central Council for Physical Recreation, SPRITO.

Answer

These are governing bodies and international organisations. The YST, for example, is a sports agency and is responsible for the development of sport for young people. SPRITO is a resource for sports, leisure and recreation professionals wishing to progress their careers.

7   Describe the different types of funding available for sport in the UK.

Answer

Grants, subsidies, National Lottery, membership fees and sponsorship.

8   What are the benefits and drawbacks of sponsorship in sport?

Answer

Benefits of sponsorship

Benefit for the sport		Benefit for the sponsor	
Additional income	Sponsorship funding offsets costs and allows better prize money, larger-scale events and lower ticket charges. For amateur or less popular sports, sponsorship can mean the difference between survival and closure. Additional income can fund vital improvements, new equipment, facilities and other items. It can also offset the costs of league entry fees and registrations, hire of facilities and payment of referees.	Publicity	The sponsor's name will be brought to the attention of the public. An event may be named after the sponsor, or the sponsor's name will be displayed on advertising boards or on the shirts of the players. The sponsor's message will be seen on television, heard on the radio and seen in newspapers.
Raising standards	Teams may be able to attract better players, improving the quality of the side. Events will be more professionally organised. Funding can mean that athletes have access to better coaching and training, and it may allow some to become full-time athletes.	Financial	The sponsor will be able to offset their sponsorship investment against tax.
Status	Team status is improved with sponsorship. A team that is receiving sponsorship will create an image of being effective, particularly if the sponsor is large and well-known.	Image	The sponsor will be linked with a popular and healthy pastime, associated with success and linked to top names in sport.

Drawbacks of sponsorship

Drawbacks for the sport		Drawbacks for the sponsor	
Dependence	Many sports become dependent on sponsorship, particularly when it involves large sums of money. If the sponsorship deal is lost, the sport often loses followers and feels the brunt of the loss of money.	Publicity	The sponsor may consider that despite the large amount of money they have provided for the sport, they have not received sufficient publicity. Sponsorship is only successful in terms of publicity if the event or team involved attract the attention of the media.
Major-minor gap	Major event sponsorship is very different from minor event sponsorship. Football, cricket and motor racing receive high levels of media coverage and sponsorship compared with minor sports which receive little or no sponsorship and therefore little or no media coverage.	Image	A sponsor runs the risk of being linked with the image of the sport. If the sport has a bad image (because of crowd behaviour, for example), then that image reflects upon the sponsor.
Lack of consultation	This relates to the lack of consultation regarding a sports player's acceptance or otherwise of the sponsor. Regardless of their personal opinion, they would have to wear the logo (for example) of the sponsor.	Association	It is important to the sponsor that their association is with a successful team or sport. Association with unsuccessful teams can be damaging to a business.

9 What is meant by racism, sexism and ageism in sport? Give examples.

Answer

- Racism – this entails discriminating against someone or acting against their best interests because of their racial background. Most sports are determined to stamp out any racist activities, for example black participants not being permitted to join a club.
- Sexism – this is about discriminating against people because of their gender, for example females not having equal playing rights in certain golf clubs.
- Ageism – this is discriminating against someone because of their age, for example a health club failing to put on activities or classes suitable for their older clientele.

10 What are the advantages and disadvantages of the influence of the media on sport?

Answer

The media has influenced the scheduling of many sporting events, including football matches and the Olympic Games. Rules have been adapted, such as video replays in cricket. Media involvement has influenced the amount of sponsorship and advertising revenue. The media can have a positive impact in as much as it encourages people to become actively involved in sports, such as the increased use of tennis courts after Wimbledon.

CHAPTER 1 – The sports industry

SPORTS, SPORTS PARTICIPATION AND SPORTS DEVELOPMENT

CASE STUDY 1.1
NEW DUTCH CLUB FOR DAVID LLOYD LEISURE

David Lloyd Leisure has opened its sixth Dutch club in an Amsterdam city centre location. His five other Dutch clubs, acquired from Cannons in late 2003, are already operating in the Netherlands, with regional director Thijs Merks at the helm. The club has been built in a high-profile building, formerly a Porsche garage, and is on a main road entering the city from the west.

The total surface area of the club is 3200 square metres, and facilities include an indoor swimming pool (24 m × 11 m) and a spa area including sauna, sunbeds and a steam room. There are around 200 pieces of state-of-the-art fitness equipment, two large studios and a massage area. In keeping with the Dutch passion for cycling, the group cycling area is larger than the UK equivalent, with 40 bikes set up. The fact that the club is situated in the city centre means that it only needs to provide basic refreshment facilities, including a coffee bar serving sandwiches and cakes. Following the successful introduction in the UK of Internet café areas with four stations within the David Lloyd Leisure clubs, this is a planned development in the near future in the new Dutch club.

The regional director of the Dutch club said of the new opening:

'We have enjoyed a fantastic response to the new club from the local community. Largely thanks to the excellent team of 40 already working hard at the club, but also due to the extensive facilities and great location, we will be opening the club with many more members than we forecast.'

David Lloyd Leisure is also planning a seventh Dutch club, this time in Rotterdam.

QUESTIONS AND TASKS

1. Who is David Lloyd and what are his main areas of expertise in sport and leisure?

    Answer ....
    ....
    ....
    ....

2. The Dutch leisure centres have large cycling areas as the Dutch enjoy cycling. What could be set up in a leisure centre specifically to cater for UK tastes?

    Answer ....
    ....
    ....
    ....

continued →

BTEC First Sport Tutor Support Pack © Jon Sutherland, Nelson Thornes Ltd, 2005

CASE STUDY 1.1 continued

3. Visit the David Lloyd Leisure Group web site at www.davidlloydleisure.co.uk and find out how many leisure centres they have in the UK.

   Answer ....

   ....

   ....

4. What is a constant feature of all the David Lloyd Leisure clubs?

   Answer ....

   ....

   ....

   ....

CHAPTER 1 – The sports industry

SPORTS, SPORTS PARTICIPATION AND SPORTS DEVELOPMENT

CASE STUDY 1.2
GROWTH OF HEALTH CLUBS IN SCOTLAND

Scotland is experiencing growth in health clubs across the country. The Hilton-owned LivingWell network of centres in Scotland is regularly packed from early morning and membership increased to 61 per cent in the three years to 2004. Since 1998 the chain of health clubs has spent £20 million in an attempt to increase the interest in health and fitness in Scotland. A premier site in Perth was opened due to the success of their club in Inverness, which opened the previous year.

Believing that their policies of employing older members of staff and not requiring users to have long-term contracts have assisted in their rise to popularity, they are, however, aware that there is increasing competition, both from the privately owned health clubs and from local authority-owned establishments.

Analysts agree that the sector is popular, with membership up 21 per cent overall and the number of private fitness centres up 6 per cent. Each private club has increased their membership by up to 200 customers, offering healthy-living disciplines including exercise, stress management, saunas, nutrition classes and beauty therapy.

Older people are also a growing aspect of the health market. People are generally living longer and older people have more time on their hands to take care of their health. Mike Balfour, the managing director of Fitness First, is reported as saying that he believes the market for health clubs is huge.

QUESTIONS AND TASKS

1   Why have the LivingWell centres spent £20 million since 1998 to increase the interest in health and fitness in Scotland?

    Answer ....

    ....

    ....

2   Visit the LivingWell web site at www.livingwell.com and find out how many clubs they have in the UK and the rest of the world.

    Answer ....

    ....

    ....

3   In which countries other than the UK have the group established health clubs?

    Answer ....

    ....

    ....

4   Print off a copy of their latest press release related to their UK clubs.

CASE STUDY 1.3
SPORT FOR ALL IN EAST KILBRIDE

Shopping bags made way for sports bags, crash mats and rowing machines as the Sport for All event kicked off at East Kilbride Shopping Centre. Shoppers inspired to get fit by the Athens Olympics had the opportunity to learn about a range of sports including gymnastics, athletics, American football and roller hockey, while instructors from local sports clubs were available to give advice on a range of healthy living issues.

Organised in conjunction with the East Kilbride Sports Council, the event was part of an ongoing programme of community-based events at Scotland's largest undercover shopping centre. By bringing a range of sports clubs into the centre, the aim of the event was to make shoppers aware of the sporting opportunities available in East Kilbride.

QUESTIONS AND TASKS

1 What is the Sport for All initiative and how is it funded?

   Answer ....

2 Why might the government be interested in encouraging people to take up sport?

   Answer ....

3 Visit the Department for Education and Skills web site at www.standards.dfes.gov.uk/specialistschools/what_are/sports/ and find out what a sports college is and how many there are operating in England.

   Answer ....

CHAPTER 1 – The sports industry

SPORTS, SPORTS PARTICIPATION AND SPORTS DEVELOPMENT

CASE STUDY 1.4
YOUTH DEVELOPMENT OFFICERS

The youth development officer posts are a result of a £1.6 million injection in the local game (i.e. football) by the Department of Culture, Arts and Leisure. The money was granted to the Northern Ireland Sports Council who made the appointments along with the Irish FA. The officers are each attached to a local club. Four regional managers will oversee the spending of the £1.6 million. Their work will include areas such as football in the community, mini-soccer and schools of excellence. Youth development officers will visit local schools and youth clubs and arrange coaching sessions to make the pupils feel that they are a part of their local football club.

The mini-soccer sessions are aimed at improving the skills of young people who are already playing the game, the emphasis being on how to use the ball, control it, pass it and shoot.

The schools of excellence are a longer-term project and the youth development officers will be aiming to develop the skills of talented young players from the age of 14 upwards by providing additional coaching.

QUESTIONS AND TASKS

1   What is the Sports Council?

    Answer ....
    ....
    ....
    ....
    ....

2   How might mini-soccer sessions assist the development of the skills of talented young players?

    Answer ....
    ....
    ....
    ....
    ....

3   What is a school of excellence?

    Answer ....
    ....
    ....
    ....
    ....

CHAPTER 1 – The sports industry

ORGANISATION OF SPORT

CASE STUDY 1.5
GOVERNING BODIES OF SPORT

The Sports Council for Northern Ireland works closely with the governing bodies of sport in Northern Ireland. The Council's role is to provide advice and guidance to assist governing bodies with the management of their sports, including such areas as strategic planning, sourcing funding, employment matters and good practice in a range of areas.

In undertaking this role, the Sports Council organises courses and seminars identified to meet the needs of governing bodies. Over the past year, the Sports Council has invested approximately £0.75 million in governing body programmes. This investment has enabled:

- the employment of staff
- the training and education of coaches, officials and administrators
- the organisation of participation programmes
- the preparation of talented performers for competitive events.

There are currently 79 governing bodies recognised by the Sports Council for Northern Ireland:

- 13 of these are Northern Ireland based governing bodies, for example the Irish Football Association and Netball Northern Ireland.
- 35 are branches of Irish governing bodies, for example the Ulster Council GAA and the Ulster Branch of Tennis Ireland.
- 31 are branches of UK governing bodies, for example the Northern Ireland Athletics Federation and the Northern Ireland Judo Federation.

QUESTIONS AND TASKS

1. The Sports Council for Northern Ireland recognises 79 different governing bodies. Find out the names of at least five of these governing bodies.

   Answer ....

   ....

2. According to the Northern Ireland Sports Council, 72 per cent of 16–19-year-olds participate in a sport. Visit www.sportni.net and find out which are the three most popular activities.

   Answer ....

   ....

3. Give five reasons why sport improves peoples' quality of life, as outlined on the web site.

   Answer ....

   ....

CHAPTER 1 – The sports industry

ORGANISATION OF SPORT

CASE STUDY 1.6
SUPPORT LOCAL SPORT INITIATIVE

The Support Local Sport Initiative is a new programme being put together by sports people for those interested in sport. The idea is to bring together participating clubs within a national programme to allow them access to centrally provided resources.

At the heart of the Support Local Sport Initiative is the concept of a Club Membership scheme, which is designed to provide a product that can be sold by a participating club on the basis that each club member is getting excellent value for money for a product they find appealing.

The scheme draws together a series of resources that allows each participating club to offer valuable benefits to club members, who would pay an annual subscription. These benefits include:

- discounts from a range of local retailers
- membership of their club's Membership Discount Scheme
- any other benefits offered directly to the club, for example discounted admission to matches.

The Support Local Sport Initiative is sponsored by local industry. Local firms reach agreement with a range of national retailers, manufacturers and service providers to offer discounts to participating club members on presentation of their membership card. Participating businesses display the Support Local Sport logo in their shop windows or on their web sites.

QUESTIONS AND TASKS

1. Why is funding from initiatives such as this important for many sports clubs?

    Answer ....
    ....
    ....

2. Visit the Support Local Sport web site at www.supportlocalsport.co.uk. What is the annual subscription fee for each club member?

    Answer ....
    ....
    ....

3. What do members receive as benefits for their annual subscription fee?

    Answer ....
    ....
    ....

CHAPTER 1 – The sports industry

ORGANISATION OF SPORT

CASE STUDY 1.7
PERSONAL TRAINING ADVERTISEMENT

Anyone wishing to improve his or her health and fitness would benefit from some time with a personal trainer. People new to exercise will quickly improve their confidence and ensure exercises are performed correctly, so results will be achieved much faster.

Someone already training will also benefit, as a personal trainer can help overcome any training plateaus and give the extra motivation needed.

Personal training is available in either a trial pack of three sessions or a full 10-session course. Personal training courses can be paid for by direct debit.

Our personal training solutions include:

- Reduce – for those wanting to lose weight safely and effectively through exercise and nutritional guidance.
- Reshape – for those wishing to transform their body shape and have a fitter, leaner and more sculpted look.
- Rematch – for those wanting to improve speed, power and co-ordination.
- Refresh – for those wanting to learn to swim.
- Refreshed – for those wanting to improve their swimming technique and level of fitness.

Why not ask one of the trainers at your local club for more information about how to get started?

QUESTIONS AND TASKS

1. Read the case study and decide what kind of qualities a personal trainer needs.

   Answer ....

   ....

   ....

2. Find the address and contact details of a local business or organisation that provides personal training courses in your area.

   Answer ....

   ....

   ....

3. Find out about the Diploma in Personal Training. How long is the course and how many modules are involved?

   Answer ....

   ....

   ....

ORGANISATION OF SPORT

CHAPTER 1 – The sports industry

ORGANISATION OF SPORT

CASE STUDY 1.8
NEW YEAR'S RESOLUTIONS

Most people make a New Year's resolution and 88 per cent of Americans have at least one. The majority of these resolutions relate to health and fitness. In 2001, 55 per cent of Americans promised to eat more heathily, 50 per cent resolved to exercise more and 38 per cent wanted to lose weight. Unfortunately most failed.

That is why the director of personal training for World Gym, Rafael Moret, has decided to close the World Gym personal training practice to resolution makers. He claims he will not accept anyone coming in with the idea that his or her resolution for 2005 is to get fit or lose weight.

The fitness expert and body transformation specialist claims people are setting themselves up to fail.

'If they know today that they need and want to get in shape or want to live a healthier lifestyle, why are they waiting until January 1 to start? Do they really think that a full year of bad habit will be magically undone at the stroke of midnight December 31?'

QUESTIONS AND TASKS

1. World Gym is a private business. Explain why the director would not accept anyone coming into the club on the basis of having made a New Year's resolution.

   Answer ....

2. How might eating more heathily assist people to lose weight?

   Answer ....

3. How might exercise assist people in losing weight?

   Answer ....

CHAPTER 1 – The sports industry

ORGANISATION OF SPORT

CASE STUDY 1.9
LINCOLNSHIRE VOLUNTARY SPORTS FORUM

The Lincolnshire Voluntary Sports Forum was established in order to support the voluntary sector in sport in Lincolnshire. The organisation is part of the new evolving sports structure that has been rolled out across England, with new Regional Sports Boards and Regional Sports Partnerships having greater influence nearer to the grass roots of sport. At a more local level, Lincolnshire has a new and developing County Sports Partnership with a director and team of officers, as well as the developing School Sports Colleges which are unfolding across the county.

The Voluntary Sports Forum works in partnership with key players in sport in Lincolnshire, trying to maximise the resources available to them in sport and connect the voluntary sector needs to providers. The Voluntary Sports Forum is support funded for two years (April 2004-March 2006) by the Lincolnshire Sports Partnership. For 2004–2005 it also received a grant from Lincolnshire County Council for small coaching support grants.

The Voluntary Forum is also the major award provider for volunteer sportspeople in Lincolnshire, with the County Volunteer Awards for Services to Sport. It seeks to influence regional and national sports policy and draw down voluntary-sector sport issues that are important to those at the heart of the sport.

QUESTIONS AND TASKS

1   Read the case study. What is meant by the phrase 'key players in sport'?

    Answer ....
    ....
    ....
    ....

2   What is the main purpose of the Voluntary Sports Forum?

    Answer ....
    ....
    ....
    ....

3   What are regional sports boards and regional sports partnerships?

    Answer ....
    ....
    ....
    ....

CHAPTER 1 – The sports industry

ORGANISATION OF SPORT

CASE STUDY 1.10
TYNEDALE'S SPORT AND RECREATION STRATEGY

Residents of Tynedale will be able to stay in shape and enjoy recreational activities thanks to a new open space, sport and recreation strategy for the district.

The plan will provide indoor and outdoor sports facilities as well as play and informal open space. The aim is to fund new and improved facilities for play, sport and informal recreation within Tynedale. It is intended that improvements and the introduction of new facilities will be developed over the next five years.

The funding for smaller projects will be via parish and town councils, some grant schemes and local fundraising. Larger projects will be funded from the Lottery or similar government-backed schemes. The council has recently appointed a leisure and cultural services officer to assist communities to develop schemes, along with the community development officer and parks and open spaces officer. One Tynedale Council official said:

'It is important that we play a key role in enabling and supporting local organisations in developing recreational and sporting facilities within their area. By improving existing facilities and providing new ones we hope to offer local communities the opportunity to engage in exercise and in sporting and play activities.'

QUESTIONS AND TASKS

1. Tynedale is a part of Northumberland. It is typical of local councils that provide a range of services. Find out what sports facilities are offered by your local council.

   Answer ....

2. How does the local council publicise its sport and recreational facilities in your local area?

   Answer ....

CHAPTER 1 – The sports industry

SOURCES OF FUNDING

CASE STUDY 1.11
SHOOTERS BRACED FOR FUNDING FIGHT

John Leighton-Dyson is urging UK Sport bosses to give his shooting team time to deliver more Olympic success and not slash their funding. UK Sport is deciding how to divide the £98 million available for the nation's athletes before the Olympic Games in China. UK Sport is responsible for distributing public money – including National Lottery cash – and is working with a proposed funding model which awards sports points for medals through to eighth-place finishes. Those who underperformed in Greece will not do so well in the distribution of the budget.

Leighton-Dyson must convince UK Sport that there are potential 2008 and 2012 medal winners among the ranks. They could learn the outcome in January 2005.

It has also been claimed that Britain's gymnasts could have their budget reduced by 95 per cent from £928,000 to £48,000. Judo has also been linked with cuts.

£98 million has been allocated for the 2008 Olympic Games, which is £8 million more than the 2004 budget for Athens. Sports such as archery, rowing, cycling and sailing, all of which were successful in Athens, could see their funding increased. It has been reported that archery could have a budget of £190,000 compared with £60,000 in 2004.

QUESTIONS AND TASKS

1. How might the way that UK Sport decides to distribute the National Lottery funding affect smaller or less-popular sporting activities?

    Answer ....
    ....
    ....
    ....
    ....
    ....
    ....

2. Visit the UK Sport web site at www.uksport.gov.uk and find out how the National Lottery money was distributed for the forthcoming Olympics in China.

    Answer ....
    ....
    ....
    ....
    ....
    ....
    ....

CHAPTER 1 – The sports industry

SOURCES OF FUNDING

CASE STUDY 1.12
TV FUNDING

Before the start of the 2004 football season, Britain's Premiership League was in negotiations with the European Commission regarding Sky's rights to all live Premiership games.

The European Commission claimed that the best interests of the consumer had not been served, although the Premier League disagreed.

It was a widely held belief that if Sky had to give away some of the rights to one of its competitors, the value of the package to football clubs would fall as Sky paid good money for the exclusive rights to televise the games. This would have affected the revenues of the clubs. The bigger clubs would probably have survived, but the smaller ones would have struggled to survive.

QUESTIONS AND TASKS

1. Find out what happened about the Sky Premiership football deal.

   Answer ....

2. How long does their current contract with the Premiership last and how many live games are screened each year?

   Answer ....

3. Why might it be in the best interests of football fans for Sky not to be the only broadcaster that can screen live matches?

   Answer ....

CHAPTER 1 – The sports industry

SOURCES OF FUNDING

CASE STUDY 1.13
SPONSORSHIP FOR THE OWLS

Sheffield Wednesday Football Club has secured a new sponsorship deal to begin at the start of next season. The club has agreed a two-year deal with the Sheffield-based Internet service provider PlusNet. The deal is said to be worth an annual six-figure sum, which will include sponsorship rights on the team shirts.

QUESTIONS AND TASKS

1. What are the advantages to PlusNet of sponsoring Sheffield Wednesday?

   Answer ....

2. What are the advantages to Sheffield Wednesday of PlusNet sponsorship?

   Answer ....

CHAPTER 1 – The sports industry

SOURCES OF FUNDING

CASE STUDY 1.14
FUNDING PROBLEM FOR BRITAIN'S SAILORS

The British team's chances of competing in the 2007 America's Cup is in doubt after it has been disclosed that they have been unable to secure a sponsorship deal.

Businessman Peter Harrison has suspended operations in Cowes and given his development team notice after failing to find a sponsor to back the team. Peter Harrison provided £28 million for the Auckland America's Cup in 2002 and had pledged £20 million for the Valencia 2007 Cup. Some smaller sponsors had been found, but the major one, HSBC, backed out at the last minute, leaving the team very short of funds.

It now looks as if Britain will not be able to compete in the America's Cup in Valencia in 2007, particularly as the final date for entries is in April 2005. Peter Harrison said:

'We have spent 18 months promoting the team and the event and we had hoped that we would have attracted major corporate backing by now to enable us to compete at the highest level. It is a tragedy that Britain may not be part of the America's Cup when the race was returning to Europe for only the second time in its history.'

QUESTIONS AND TASKS

1   Find out what has happened about the sponsorship for the British team with regard to the America's Cup in Valencia in 2007, bearing in mind that the team had to prove its sponsorship before April 2005.

    Answer ....
    ....
    ....
    ....
    ....
    ....

CHAPTER 1 – The sports industry

SOURCES OF FUNDING

CASE STUDY 1.15
SWANSEA SPONSORSHIP DEAL

Swansea City Football Club has announced a one-year shirt-sponsorship deal with RE/MAX estate agency. The contract is for the 2004/2005 season and will have the option of continuing for a further year. The club is delighted with the deal and hopes it will encourage fans to frequent the estate agent. It is considered to be an exciting partnership and one that promotes the club by its affiliation with a major brand name.

QUESTIONS AND TASKS

1   Visit the official Swansea City Football Club web site (www.swanseacity.premiumtv.co.uk/page/Home) and find out the full range of different businesses which have sponsorship deals with the club. Click on the banner advertisements for each of the sponsors and briefly note what each of the businesses do.

    Answer ....
    ....
    ....
    ....
    ....
    ....

KEY ISSUES AND THE INFLUENCE OF THE MEDIA

CASE STUDY 1.16
RACISM ON THE PITCH

Birmingham player, Dwight Yorke, alleged he was subjected to racist abuse while warming up during the match at his former club Blackburn. This incident came less than a week after racist chanting was heard during England's friendly match in Spain.

There was some discussion about whether or not the players should walk off the field if the racism continued, but the players decided they wanted to stay and convince supporters of their ability.

A survey carried out by the Commission for Racial Equality found that football's authorities and clubs do not take racism seriously and that ethnic minorities are under-represented in the non-playing side of the game.

The level of racism in English football is much less than 10 or 20 years ago, although there are only three black managers in the game at the present time.

There is to be an initiative between the League Managers' Association, the Premier League, the Football Association and the Football League to ensure equality on the coaching and management side, where the numbers are disproportionate.

QUESTIONS AND TASKS

1. Find out more about the Commission for Racial Equality's investigation into racism in football. Visit the CRE web site at www.cre.gov.uk/.
   What are their findings and what do they suggest?

   Answer ....

CHAPTER 1 – The sports industry

KEY ISSUES AND THE INFLUENCE OF THE MEDIA

CASE STUDY 1.17
ADRIAN MUTU

Romanian Adrian Mutu, the former Chelsea player, was suspended from the club in November 2004 for taking cocaine. His suspension lasts until May 2005, but he will not be allowed to resume playing until he has undergone rehabilitation at Sporting Chance, a charity that was set up to help sportsmen and women to overcome their addictions.

His rehabilitation will be supervised by his mentor, Tony Adams, who himself overcame an addiction. Mutu claimed he was driven to cocaine during the strain of a recent divorce and estrangement from his children, but that he only used the drug on four or five occasions.

QUESTIONS AND TASKS

1 What is the Sporting Chance Clinic?

   Answer ....

   ....

   ....

   ....

   ....

   ....

2 Who set up the clinic and when was it founded?

   Answer ....

   ....

   ....

   ....

   ....

   ....

CHAPTER 1 – The sports industry

KEY ISSUES AND THE INFLUENCE OF THE MEDIA

CASE STUDY 1.18
REAL MADRID FINE

Real Madrid Football Club have been fined nearly £7000 as a result of their fans displaying racist behaviour at a Champions League match in November 2004. UEFA's imposed fine took into account the fact that this racist behaviour had not occurred before in Real Madrid's crowd.

The Italian side Lazio also experienced racist crowd behaviour and as a result have been forced to play their European games excluding their fans. Lazio have been fined three times for racist behaviour by their fans, as well as missile throwing and clashes with Italian police.

QUESTIONS AND TASKS

1 Find out about the Real Madrid fine and their reaction to it.

   Answer ....

2 What was Lazio's reaction to the action taken against them?

   Answer ....

KEY ISSUES AND THE INFLUENCE OF THE MEDIA

CASE STUDY 1.19
BECKHAM AT REAL MADRID

On his first day as a Real Madrid player, David Beckham broke all records for shirt sales. The main souvenir shop alongside the Real Madrid stadium sold 8000 shirts with the number 23 on the back in just over seven hours. Two hundred were sold in the first hour after Beckham received his new jersey, but sales rocketed once the news spread that the shirts were in stock in the souvenir shop.

The sale of Beckham shirts put those of Ronaldo, Zidane and Figo to shame.

The Real Madrid president, Florentino Perez, has admitted that he signed David Beckham as much for his celebrity fame and commercial power as for his ability to play football. Perez is hopeful that Beckham's signing fee will be covered by the sale of number 23 shirts in Asia, where Beckham is more a fashion than a sporting icon.

QUESTIONS AND TASKS

1. What is the value to Real Madrid of Beckham's name on their shirts? Try to find out how many shirts are being sold by the club each year.

   Answer ....
   ....
   ....
   ....
   ....
   ....
   ....

CHAPTER 1 – The sports industry

KEY ISSUES AND THE INFLUENCE OF THE MEDIA

CASE STUDY 1.20
CARLING CUP VIOLENCE

Liverpool and Millwall fans have blamed one another for the violence that occurred at the Carling Cup match in October 2004, where 68 seats were ripped out in the visitors' section. Three Liverpool supporters and one Millwall fan were ejected from the stadium and the Football Association has confirmed that investigations will be carried out. Police used riot gear to prevent Liverpool supporters from invading the pitch and one disabled supporter was injured in the melee. The Football Association intends to speak to both clubs and to the police, as well as the referee. Football's governing body told reporters that they could not give an indication of the timescale involved, but they would seek to get as much information as possible.

QUESTIONS AND TASKS

1 Find out what happened about this incident. What action was taken against the clubs and supporters?

   Answer ....

CHAPTER 1 – The sports industry

IVA REVISION AND PREPARATION

Students will need to prepare the following to meet the grading criteria of this unit:

- A definition of sport.
- A list of sporting activities available locally and nationally.
- A summary of how sport is organised in the UK, with examples from the public, private and voluntary sectors.
- A list of reasons why people participate in sport and why they may *not* involve themselves in sport.
- A list of the different ways in which sport is funded, including different forms of sponsorship.
- A list and explanations of the key issues affecting sport.
- A list of ways in which the mass media influences two sports.

ANSWERS AND GUIDELINES TO CASE STUDY 1.1

1. David Lloyd was a successful British tennis player.
2. Aerobics or five-a-side football. There are a host of other potential suggestions.
3. At the time of writing the group had 57 leisure centres in the UK, the first having been established in 1982.
4. The constant feature of all of the leisure centres is the inclusion of tennis-based activities and training.

ANSWERS AND GUIDELINES TO CASE STUDY 1.2

1. As the business is one of the leading companies providing this service in Scotland they have a vested interest in encouraging people to join health clubs.
2. At the time of writing the group had 85 clubs in the UK and 10 worldwide.
3. At the time of writing they had clubs in Germany, Malta, Turkey, Australia and Brazil.
4. Students will be able to find this information by clicking on the 'press office' and selecting 'recent press releases'.

ANSWERS AND GUIDELINES TO CASE STUDY 1.3

1. It is a government initiative to encourage people to play sports and it is funded by the National Lottery.
2. The government is concerned about pressures on the NHS, particularly with regard to what is perceived to be a largely unfit and overweight population. They are positively encouraging the public to become involved in sports in order to help combat these two issues.
3. At the time of writing there were 228 sports colleges in England, operating as part of the Specialist Schools Programme. The web site provides a link to show the spread of schools and colleges around the country, which have a specialism in sport. At the time of writing the revised list included 266 centres.

ANSWERS AND GUIDELINES TO CASE STUDY 1.4

1. The English Sports Council is also known as Sport England. It is directly involved in creating opportunities for people to start in sport then remain in sport. It encourages people to get involved in sport and physical recreation activities. Further information can be found at www.sportengland.org.
2. Since the mini-soccer sessions are being run in conjunction with local football clubs, the hope is that talented youngsters can be spotted by the clubs and offered longer-term training and assistance in improving their soccer skills. It also provides the youngsters with a taster of real soccer training by professionals.
3. Schools of Excellence exist in both the public and the private sector, such as the FA's National School of Football Excellence at Lilleshall or the Bobby Charlton School of Football Excellence.

ANSWERS AND GUIDELINES TO CASE STUDY 1.5

1. By clicking on 'links' on the Northern Ireland Sports Council web site a full list of governing bodies can be found, broken down into NI/Ulster, GB/UK, Irish, World/Euro and other sporting bodies.
2. The three most popular activities are walking, swimming and keep fit.
3. The five reasons given are:
   (a) improved sense of pride, both locally and nationally;
   (b) that young people place an importance on sport in their lives;
   (c) that Northern Ireland has a far healthier population than most of the rest of the UK;
   (d) that people who are involved in sport for three-quarters of their lives have a lower

incidence of heart disease, angina or breathlessness; and

(e) people active in sport have lower coronary risks.

ANSWERS AND GUIDELINES TO CASE STUDY 1.6

1. Many clubs have to rely on their membership in order to survive. Gate receipts are relatively low and any commercial venture with local or national businesses can prove to be of vital importance to the success and survival of the club.
2. The annual subscription fee is £25 at the time of writing.
3. Members receive discounts from a range of local retailers, membership of the club's discount scheme and other benefits such as discounted admission to matches.

ANSWERS AND GUIDELINES TO CASE STUDY 1.7

1. The individual needs to be outgoing, friendly, have good communication skills and be a good all-round organiser. The individual needs to be certified to ensure that standards are maintained and that any qualifications are accredited.
2. A good starting point is the National Register of Personal Trainers, which can be found at www.nrpt.co.uk. Students can search for trainers or find more information about how to become a trainer, as well as discovering where training courses are held. Examples include fitness industry education, Future Fit training, and premier training and YMCA fitness industry training.
3. The diploma is widely recognised as an entry standard into the health and fitness industry. It provides learners with a Level 3 qualification and is nationally recognised, accredited and acknowledged by all major health clubs. Usually it is a 12-week course, consisting of fitness instruction, fitness training and sports massage.

ANSWERS AND GUIDELINES TO CASE STUDY 1.8

1. A discussion could revolve around the fact that many private health clubs are judged on their successes and failures. An individual who approaches the club solely with a resolution in mind may not be as motivated and may be more likely to fail, thereby damaging the club's reputation.
2. Healthy eating involves regulating the intake of fats and carbohydrates in accordance with the body's needs, as well as improving the overall nutritional value of the food. Healthier eating may lead to reduced consumption of fats and carbohydrates, which will lead to eventual, if gradual, weight loss.
3. Exercise will accelerate the weight-loss process.

ANSWERS AND GUIDELINES TO CASE STUDY 1.9

1. The key players in sport are the main clubs and governing bodies, which either provide facilities or a framework and guidance for sports in the UK.
2. The main purpose of the Voluntary Sports Forum is to maximise the resources of the voluntary sector by helping them to access funding and resources. They also seek to influence regional and national sports policies.
3. Regional sports boards are the organisations through which Sport England distributes its funding to areas of the UK. Regional sports partnerships are another tier related to Sport England, which provide assistance and support to the regional sports boards. There are nine regional sports boards.

ANSWERS AND GUIDELINES TO CASE STUDY 1.10

This set of activities can be easily achieved by either visiting the local council and asking for a leaflet on sports and leisure facilities owned by the council, or by searching for the relevant council's web site. The web site should contain a listing of the facilities offered by the council and perhaps additional links to particular centres in the area.

ANSWERS AND GUIDELINES TO CASE STUDY 1.11

1. The funding mechanism pays out to different sports based on medals and top eight placings. Therefore sports with few competitors are unlikely to attract a large amount of funding. Equally, if a sport has a blip in its results and under-achieves then it is penalised for the next Olympics as less athletes are supported under the World Class Performance Programme. For example, for Athens, athletics had 64 athletes while weightlifting, at the other end of the scale, had just one.
2. The sport funding guide should be available on this web site from January 2005. There will be a

summary of the funding guide showing the Lottery funding committed and the total amount allocated for the Olympics in China.

ANSWERS AND GUIDELINES TO CASE STUDY 1.12

1. At the time of writing, the situation was still in dispute, but the EU was claiming that at least one other broadcaster should be allowed to screen live matches.

2. The current deal is due to finish in 2007. They show around 60 live games per season.

3. Generally it is thought that Sky holding a virtual monopoly on satellite broadcasting is not in the best interests of the general public. In order to access live football via Sky, viewers have to purchase a general Sky package and pay to view each game. Those who cannot afford this are disadvantaged, and Sky can charge whatever they want because of the lack of competition.

ANSWERS AND GUIDELINES TO CASE STUDY 1.13

1. The total value of shirt sponsorship in Europe during the 2002/03 season was over £226 million. The key advantages to businesses of being involved in this kind of marketing are that their name is seen by hundreds of thousands, if not millions, of potential customers. Businesses look for opportunities to link with high-profile football teams, particularly those that will be involved in televised matches.

2. As far as the teams are concerned, these deals provide vital additional income. The payments to clubs such as Bayern Munich can be worth over £11 million per year. Manchester United's deal with Vodafone is worth £9 million a year. This income underwrites many of the player-related expenses of the club.

ANSWERS AND GUIDELINES TO CASE STUDY 1.14

1. Useful places for students to begin their research are:
   (a) www.americascup.com/en/
   (b) www.americascupnews.com/
   (c) www.eurosport.com (choose 'other' from the menu and select 'sailing')

ANSWERS AND GUIDELINES TO CASE STUDY 1.15

1. At the time of writing, the following businesses had sponsorship arrangements with the club:
   (a) www.encoreswanseabay.co.uk/
   (b) www.swanstrust.com/
   (c) www.remax-wales.com/
   (d) www.home.ntl.com/icat/familypack
   (e) Coca-Cola
   (f) Nationwide.

ANSWERS AND GUIDELINES TO CASE STUDY 1.16

1. According to the press release:

   'Every member of the FA board and the 92-strong FA council is white, but this is the typical picture in the footballing world. The report looks at the extent of racial discrimination in the non-playing side of football and an action plan has been devised to secure change.

   The multi-million pound football industry thrives on the skills of players from all ethnic backgrounds. Yet non-white faces make up less than 1 per cent of positions off the field, whether in boardrooms, management or the coaching staff – and less than 2 per cent of supporters on the terraces. The report found that 75 per cent of football clubs have informal recruitment practices – 'if your face fits, you get the job.'

   The main findings include:
   (a) ethnic minorities are severely under-represented in the non-playing side of football (board membership, coaching, training and other aspects of the administration and management) as well as on the terraces;
   (b) there are hardly any Asian or Chinese players at any level or in any age group;
   (c) the majority of professional football league clubs do not give their staff equal opportunities training. Many clubs still have no equal opportunities policy and where this does exist it is very basic.

   The CRE action plan requires:
   (a) organisations to adopt an equal opportunities policy and implementation plan by July 2005;
   (b) all organisations to review recruitment and selection by January 2006;

(c) all organisations to tackle under-representation and develop representative strategies by July 2006;

(d) the FA and All Agency Review Team to evaluate equal opportunities policies and provide further support to clubs.

A full copy of the report can be found at www.cre.gov.uk/pdfs/football_report_full.pdf.

ANSWERS AND GUIDELINES TO CASE STUDY 1.17

1. 'The aim is to provide a safe environment where the addict can begin a new life free from the drug or behaviour pattern that has been damaging them, their families and their sporting life. The philosophy is based on Tony's own experiences of his requirements as an athlete in his own recovery from alcoholism: the unity of mind, body and spirit.'

2. 'Sporting Chance Clinic was formed in September 2000 by the former Arsenal and England captain, Tony Adams MBE, and is a registered charity dedicated to providing support, counselling, treatment and aftercare to sportsmen and women who are suffering from addictive illnesses such as alcoholism, drug abuse, compulsive gambling and eating disorders, with all their side-effects including anxiety and depression.'

The web site can be found at www.sportingchancecharity.com/.

ANSWERS AND GUIDELINES TO CASE STUDY 1.18

1. At the time of writing (December 2004), the situation regarding Real Madrid was:

   (a) Real Madrid confirmed that they will launch an appeal against the fine imposed on them by UEFA;

   (b) the Spanish giants were handed a fine of just under €10,000 euros for racist chanting during the Champions League match against Bayer Leverkusen at the Bernabeu on 23 November 2004;

   (c) the club said: 'Real Madrid consider themselves a club that has always proved to have an impeccable attitude in the fight against racism';

   (d) they went on to say: 'Regardless of the small quantity of the fine, Real Madrid consider that this has been a minimal incident; that the ones responsible are not regular spectators at the club's games and are in fact of Romanian nationality. Real Madrid wants to point out that the Bernabeu is a stadium where these situations don't happen often.'

2. The situation regarding Lazio, again at the time of writing, was:

   (a) UEFA's control and disciplinary body has punished the Rome club with a stadium ban following racist abuse and crowd disturbances – including missile throwing and flares being set off, clashes with police and a stabbing incident – during the UEFA Cup match against FK Partizan on 25 November 2004;

   (b) Lazio, who have now been penalised three times for racism offences, have completed their fixtures in this season's competition, meaning the ban will carry over until they next qualify for a UEFA club competition. Partizan, meanwhile, were fined €5200 after their fans threw flares during the 2–2 draw at the Stadio Olimpico.

ANSWERS AND GUIDELINES TO CASE STUDY 1.19

1. According to the club at the time of signing Beckham (summer 2003), Real Madrid were set to recoup the £17 million they had already spent on David Beckham before he even kicked a ball in anger. Their jackpot saw the England skipper virtually paid for by the time the Primera Liga season kicked off in September 2003. The Spanish giants paid Manchester United £17 million for his services plus an extra £8 million based on bonuses that depended on Real's Champions League progress. They made £8 million from their four-match Far East Tour in August 2003. Worldwide sales of Beckham shirts are expected to bring in an incredible £35 million over the four years of his contract – around £8.75 million a year.

ANSWERS AND GUIDELINES TO CASE STUDY 1.20

1. As of 10 December 2004, the situation was as follows:

   (a) the Football Association charged Liverpool and Millwall over crowd trouble during their Carling Cup match on 26 October. Millwall, who lost the match 3–0, are the first club to be charged by the FA over racist behaviour by their fans;

(b) the disciplinary action relates to alleged abuse aimed at Liverpool's French defender Djimi Traore. In addition, four people were ejected from Millwall's stadium, seats were thrown and a disabled fan was injured.

As a result, Millwall have been charged with failing to ensure that fans refrained from racist and/or abusive behaviour and for failing to prevent spectators throwing missiles onto the pitch;

(c) Millwall chairman Theo Paphitis, said:

'God knows what the FA are up to. There was never any indication of racist abuse being brought into the discussions. The charges are completely ridiculous and we'll see what evidence the FA has got to back them up. It just seems like the FA is a rudderless ship at the moment and is seeking publicity for its own aim. Racism is too important a subject to use to point score.'

(d) Liverpool have been charged with one breach for failing to prevent their fans' threatening and/or violent and/or provocative behaviour. Liverpool fans claimed the trouble was sparked by Millwall supporters' chants about the Hillsborough disaster, where 96 people were crushed to death in April 1989.

Theo Paphitis has denied this and said CCTV footage showed that the catalyst for the trouble was a Liverpool fan attacking a Millwall fan in the west stand. Both clubs had until 23 December to respond to the charges.

CHAPTER 2
Health, safety and injury

The information on this page is intended to help you plan and deliver your lessons using BTEC First Sport *by John Honeybourne.*

OVERVIEW

This is the second compulsory core chapter and its content underpins many of the other chapters. It looks at the element of risk taken by participants in sport and the awareness needed to ensure the safety of others. The chapter also looks at common injuries and risk assessment. The main goals of the chapter are:

- To look at the main risks in sports participation and how injuries can be prevented or minimised.
- To examine the common types of injuries and how these can be treated.
- To create a risk assessment for a participant sports activity.

ADVICE AND GUIDANCE TO STUDENTS

Students need to look at the risks of injury and the types and treatment of injuries, as well as investigating and identifying the risks relating to a particular sports activity. In order to understand the full demands of the IVA, it is useful to appreciate exactly what the tutor will be looking for. A detailed view of this is shown in the following table:

PASS	To obtain a MERIT do this as well	To obtain a DISTINCTION do this as well
Identify injuries and risks to participants in four different sporting activities.	Explain how these injuries and risks could affect the participants.	Compare the injuries and risks and how they affect performance.
With tutor support, describe common injuries and their treatment.	Do it independently and choose a sport or activity, explaining laws, rules and regulations.	Evaluate the risks, suggest health and safety issues and offer alternatives to the standard treatments.
With tutor support, assess the level of need for two different injuries and carry out a risk assessment on a selected sport or activity.	Do this independently and cover the needs for two injuries.	Analyse your checklist and evaluate its use for its target audience (the participants).

CHAPTER 2 – Health, safety and injury

SUGGESTED LESSON PLAN

TOPIC	HOURS	ACTIVITY TO USE	PAGE
Main risk factors Factors	7	Case Study 2.1 Success through starvation?	34
		Case Study 2.2 Player safety fears	35
Minimising risks	7	Case Study 2.3 Too soon to return	36
Rules and regulations	4	Case Study 2.4 Health fears	37
Common sporting injuries Types of injury	7	Case Study 2.5 Ralf Schumacher	38
		Case Study 2.6 Blair misses World Cup	39
		Case Study 2.7 Operation for Irish flanker	40
		Case Study 2.8 Dehydration	41
		Case Study 2.9 Paula Radcliffe in Athens	42
Situation assessment	7	Case Study 2.10 Rupture of the gastrocnemius or soleus muscle	43
		Case Study 2.11 Painful finger	44
		Case Study 2.12 Recurring injury	45
Alternative treatments	3	Case Study 2.13 Acupuncture	46
Checklists	2	Case Study 2.14 Merton College Oxford	47
Risk assessment Health and safety hazards	3	Case Study 2.15 Swimming pool chemical fears	48
Purpose of risk assessment	3	Case Study 2.16 Field events	49
Risk assessment and monitoring risks	10	Case Study 2.17 Pole vault and high-jump soft landing areas	51
		Case Study 2.18 Competition	52
		Case Study 2.19 Track events	53
		Case Study 2.20 Members' responsibilities	54
IVA revision and preparation	7		55

ANSWERS TO PROGRESS CHECK (PAGE 51, BTEC FIRST SPORT)

1 Name 10 of the main risks associated with sport.

Answer

The main risks are:

- poor physical fitness or inappropriate physique for the activity
- poor level of skills or technique
- lack of effective preparation (such as warming up and cooling down)
- dangerous training practices
- inadequate or inappropriate diet
- influence of alcohol or drugs
- dangerous environment (e.g. broken bottles on a playing field)
- weather conditions
- inappropriate or dangerous clothing
- lifting and carrying of equipment
- inappropriate or damaged equipment
- behaviour of other participants.

2 Choose one of the above risks and give an example of a sports activity where this may occur.

Answer

An example can be taken from the textbook, such as that given for inappropriate or damaged equipment:

'The equipment that is used in sport should also be correct for the activity and the age/ability of the sportspeople involved. For example, in gymnastics the vaulting box should be at an appropriate height; for very young novice tennis players the rackets may be lighter and smaller than full size. If the equipment is inappropriate then injury may occur. For example, if a vaulting box is too high then there is a greater chance of the gymnast colliding with it. A tennis player who

CHAPTER 2 – Health, safety and injury

has a racket that is too heavy may well suffer muscle strains in the arm. Damaged equipment can also cause injury. For example, a damaged basketball backboard may well become loose and fall on a competitor causing serious injury.'

3 List three ways of minimising the chance of an injury in sport.

Answer
Participants should ensure they are fit, they must have achieved a particular skill level and have a reasonable technique. They should carry out an effective warm-up in order to prepare for the activity.

4 What factors should be taken into account when planning a safe training programme for a sports activity of your choice?

Answer
A student's answer should include most of the following aspects of a good training programme:

- identify training goals
- identify macro-, meso- and micro-cycles
- identify fitness components needing improvement
- identify energy systems to be used
- identify muscle groups to be used
- evaluate fitness components
- use a training diary
- vary the programme to ensure motivation
- allow rest days for recovery
- evaluate and reassess goals as necessary.

5 Outline the Health and Safety at Work Act 1974.

Answer
The Act aims to secure the health, safety and welfare of individuals at work. It also aims to protect others against risks to health or safety. It has led to great improvements in sports buildings and equipment, as well as better staff working conditions.

6 Name two regulations that are included in the Control of Substances Hazardous to Health Regulations 1994.

Answer
The list for possible inclusion is:

- the creation of a code of practice
- using a trained risk assessor
- passing information to staff
- using hazardous substances only when absolutely necessary
- training staff to use personal protection and advising them on emergency procedures
- maintaining control of substances
- monitoring the handling of substances.

7 Identify three guidance points that you would make to anyone working with children in sport.

Answer
The three points could include any of the following:

- not to work alone with children
- restrict physical contact to non-sensitive areas of the body
- only use physical restraint in emergencies
- behave as an appropriate role model.

8 Name a sports injury that you or a friend has had recently. Give details of the injury and how you would treat it immediately after the injury occurred.

Answer
This question could produce a wide variety of answers, including minor abrasions, concussion, sickness, dizziness, headaches or more severe injuries such as broken bones or serious damage to muscles.

9 What factors should you take into consideration when planning a risk assessment in sport?

Answer
The key points for inclusion are:

- an identification of the health and safety hazards
- the level of risk
- the risks that are involved
- procedures for monitoring or checking the minimisation of risks.

10 Give examples of low, moderate and high hazards in sport.

Answer
A student should give examples such as the following:

- low – music player used in a yoga class
- moderate – a rugby forward playing in a rugby match
- high – canoeing in open water

MAIN RISK FACTORS

CASE STUDY 2.1
SUCCESS THROUGH STARVATION?

A recent newspaper article claimed that a jockey is in danger of doing his body serious damage by starving himself to ensure he makes the correct weight for races. The jockey's diet, according to a sports dietician, could impair his health and batter his immune system, as well as putting his organs under threat.

The dietician claimed that vitamin supplements are never sufficient to compensate for a good diet. The dietician suggests that athletes should plan for a race and in order to allow the body to adapt should reduce their weight slowly. This can be done by reducing fat, alcohol and carbohydrates, but not by crash dieting. The long-term implications of crash diets are not known, but it is known that such forms of weight loss can cause mood swings and an athlete's ability to recover from common coughs and colds.

QUESTIONS AND TASKS

Read the case study and then find out the following:

1   What is the average weight of a jockey?

    Answer ....

    ....

2   What could be done to prevent jockeys from having to lose so much weight?

    Answer ....

    ....

CHAPTER 2 – Health, safety and injury

MAIN RISK FACTORS

CASE STUDY 2.2
PLAYER SAFETY FEARS

Hibernian manager Bobby Williamson has called for Dunfermline to replace their artificial playing surface because of his fears that player safety is at risk. Williamson claims the players cannot keep their feet and there is a likelihood of a serious injury.

Dunfermline received funding from UEFA to install the experimental surface and the club has defended the pitch, although a spokesperson said there were no plans to replace it as they were not allowed to do so.

QUESTIONS AND TASKS

Read the case study about player safety on artificial pitches and then investigate the following:

1   What kind of injuries would be avoided if the playing surface was real grass?

    Answer ....

    ....

    ....

2   What are the benefits of artificial surfaces and what is the current view of UEFA on artificial surfaces?

    Answer ....

    ....

    ....

CHAPTER 2 – Health, safety and injury

MAIN RISK FACTORS

CASE STUDY 2.3
TOO SOON TO RETURN

The former World Boxing Council (WBC) bantamweight champion, Wayne McCullough's planned comeback against Uganda's John Mackay was called off. McCullough injured his left hand in training and had to withdraw from the fight. The injury was an old problem that was aggravated during a training session and although treatment was given, it failed to improve in time. The boxer's hand was still aching despite cortisone injections and he did not want to fight with a disadvantage.

QUESTIONS AND TASKS

1   Find out about the injuries sustained by Wayne McCullough over the course of his boxing career. Which injury nearly ended his career for good?

    Answer ....
    ....
    ....
    ....

CHAPTER 2 – Health, safety and injury

MAIN RISK FACTORS

CASE STUDY 2.4
HEALTH FEARS

In 2003 the World Badminton Championships, which were scheduled to be held in Birmingham, were threatened because of the SARS epidemic. Kelly Morgan, the Welsh badminton player, told newspapers that she had serious fears about health risks from SARS and the International Badminton Federations (IBF), the sport's governing body, told reporters that there was only a 50–50 chance that the championship would go ahead.

The primary concern was the inclusion of the players from the Asian continent, where the population had suffered most from the potentially fatal virus.

Malaysia's national badminton coach had also called for the competition to be cancelled.

QUESTIONS AND TASKS

1. What is the SARS epidemic?

   Answer ....
   ....
   ....
   ....
   ....

2. What might be the implications of such an epidemic to a major sporting event?

   Answer ....
   ....
   ....
   ....
   ....
   ....
   ....
   ....

CHAPTER 2 – Health, safety and injury

COMMON SPORTING INJURIES

CASE STUDY 2.5
RALF SCHUMACHER

German racing driver Ralf Schumacher missed several Grand Prix because of injuries sustained in a crash at the US Grand Prix in 2004. The two broken vertebrae sustained during the crash meant that the driver was ordered by his doctors to sit the races out. It was reported that another accident like the one in Indianapolis could be disastrous for Schumacher, who could have ended up a paraplegic, and it was decided that the driver should continue with his convalescence rather than risk racing too soon.

QUESTIONS AND TASKS

1 What might be the implications of such an injury to a racing-car driver such as Schumacher?

    Answer ....
    ....
    ....
    ....
    ....
    ....
    ....
    ....

2 What treatments could be used to help heal the two broken vertebrae?

    Answer ....
    ....
    ....
    ....
    ....
    ....
    ....
    ....

CHAPTER 2 – Health, safety and injury

COMMON SPORTING INJURIES

CASE STUDY 2.6
BLAIR MISSES WORLD CUP

Ben Blair, the 24-year-old New Zealand fullback, was sent home and replaced in the World Cup team due to a serious neck injury. After a scan the nature of the training injury was confirmed as a prolapsed disc. This occurs when the casing surrounding the disc bursts and presses against the ligaments and nerves that run close to the disc. Although the injury was not considered to be career threatening, this could have been the outcome if sensible action had not been taken to withdraw Blair from further games.

QUESTIONS AND TASKS

1. What is a prolapsed disc and what is the treatment for the complaint?

   Answer ....
   ....
   ....
   ....
   ....
   ....

2. What happened to Ben Blair after the accident?

   Answer ....
   ....
   ....
   ....
   ....
   ....
   ....

CHAPTER 2 – Health, safety and injury

COMMON SPORTING INJURIES

CASE STUDY 2.7
OPERATION FOR IRISH FLANKER

Alan Quinlan, the 29-year-old Ireland flanker, missed the Six Nations Championship because of the need for an operation on his shoulder. He suffered a dislocation and torn ligaments while playing against Argentina in the World Cup. This is a common injury among rugby players and several other internationals have had similar operations in the past. Also common in the game is a ruptured Achilles tendon, which causes the foot to be in plaster for six months following a repair operation.

QUESTIONS AND TASKS

1. What are the other common injuries for rugby players?

   Answer ....
   ....
   ....
   ....
   ....
   ....
   ....

2. How long would it take to recover from an injury such as the one suffered by Alan Quinlan?

   Answer ....
   ....
   ....

COMMON SPORTING INJURIES

CHAPTER 2 – Health, safety and injury

COMMON SPORTING INJURIES

CASE STUDY 2.8
DEHYDRATION

Tennis player Justine Henin-Hardenne was put on a drip after suffering dehydration during a three-hour, three-minute tennis match. She was forced to lie down with a drip in her arm in the medical room after experiencing cramping of her left arm when serving.

Marlon Black, the 26-year-old West Indian fast bowler, was also taken to hospital suffering from severe dehydration. He was placed on an intravenous drip and doctors assessed his condition.

QUESTIONS AND TASKS

1   What is dehydration?

    Answer ....
    ....
    ....
    ....
    ....
    ....

2   How can a sports person avoid dehydration?

    Answer ....
    ....
    ....
    ....
    ....
    ....

CHAPTER 2 – Health, safety and injury

COMMON SPORTING INJURIES

CASE STUDY 2.9
PAULA RADCLIFFE IN ATHENS

An Olympic gold medal was denied Britain's Paula Radcliffe in the Athens Olympic Games when she pulled out of the marathon after 23 miles. Thirty year-old Paula was taken to hospital by ambulance for a check-up after complaining of distress in the hot and humid conditions. It was reported after the check-up that the double London marathon winner was exhausted rather than physically injured.

QUESTIONS AND TASKS

1   What were the reasons for Paula Radcliffe's failure in the Athens marathon?

    Answer ....
    ....
    ....
    ....

2   What was the other race she had to pull out of later in the Olympics?

    Answer ....
    ....
    ....
    ....

CHAPTER 2 – Health, safety and injury

COMMON SPORTING INJURIES

CASE STUDY 2.10
RUPTURE OF THE GASTROCNEMIUS OR SOLEUS MUSCLE

Brian is a runner and he has just injured himself. His symptoms include:

- a sudden pain at the back of the leg
- difficulty in contracting the muscle or standing on tiptoe
- pain and swelling or bruising in the calf muscle.

The calf muscles consist of the gastrocnemius (the large muscle at the back of the lower leg) and the soleus muscle (a smaller muscle lower down the leg and under the gastrocnemius).

QUESTIONS AND TASKS

1. Describe Brian's problem.

   Answer ....

2. How might he and a specialist be able to solve the situation?

   Answer ....

COMMON SPORTING INJURIES

CASE STUDY 2.11
PAINFUL FINGER

Rachel has the following symptoms:

- pain over the joint in the finger where the damage has occurred
- pain when bending the finger and stressing the injured ligament
- swelling over the joint
- restricted mobility in the finger
- instability in the finger.

QUESTIONS AND TASKS

1   What is wrong with Rachel's finger?

    Answer ....
    ....
    ....
    ....
    ....

2   What can be done for her?

    Answer ....
    ....
    ....
    ....
    ....

CHAPTER 2 – Health, safety and injury

COMMON SPORTING INJURIES

CASE STUDY 2.12
RECURRING INJURY

Jose Reyes, the second baseman for the New York Mets, missed the opening game of the season after injuring his right hamstring during a training game. The problem has occurred three times in the last year, leading to him missing three games last May and five in July. Reyes told interviewers that although he knew there was a serious problem with his leg, he was unsure as to the reason for it and that further tests would have to be undertaken.

QUESTIONS AND TASKS

1. What could be done for Jose Reyes?

   Answer ....

2. What is the likely period of rest needed to deal with his complaint?

   Answer ....

CHAPTER 2 – Health, safety and injury

COMMON SPORTING INJURIES

CASE STUDY 2.13
ACUPUNCTURE

Research has shown that acupuncture triggers the release of endorphins in the brain. These chemicals affect various body systems, reduce pain and make the patient feel good. Traditionally it is thought that acupuncture removes blockages and promotes the flow of Qi energy through the meridians. This is believed to improve the functioning of the internal organs. Some researchers believe that changes in Qi energy can be measured with techniques such as Kirlian photography, which is said to take pictures of the energy field, but more proof is needed.

Thousands of acupuncture studies have been carried out worldwide. These have shown it to be effective for a wide range of ailments including asthma, headaches, menstrual problems, digestive problems, high blood pressure and pain.

QUESTIONS AND TASKS

1   What is Qi energy?

    Answer ....

    ....

    ....

    ....

    ....

    ....

2   What are endorphins?

    Answer ....

    ....

    ....

    ....

    ....

    ....

3   What is Kirlian photography?

    Answer ....

    ....

    ....

    ....

    ....

    ....

COMMON SPORTING INJURIES

CHAPTER 2 – Health, safety and injury

COMMON SPORTING INJURIES

CASE STUDY 2.14
MERTON COLLEGE OXFORD

Recording and reporting accidents

There is an accident book at the College pavilion. *Irrespective of the cause*, the circumstances of any non-trivial accident *or near miss* sustained on the premises must be recorded in the accident book by the person suffering (or narrowly avoiding) injury or by a witness, and the accident record should be returned as soon as possible to the bursar, who has overall responsibility for health and safety within the College. This is a statutory requirement.

First aid

There is a first-aid kit at the College pavilion. The captain or team leader should locate the kit, ensure it is adequately stocked and verify first-aid procedures before each fixture. If the captain or team leader is not qualified in first aid, s/he should verify whether the referee, umpire or any other person present is qualified. The groundsman is qualified in first aid, but may not be available to be summoned. The College nurse, lodge porters and other College staff are also qualified in first aid, but it would take time to summon them to the sports ground and they might not be available. First aid will normally be administered only in relatively trivial cases of injury, or in serious cases as a holding measure while the emergency services are summoned.

Serious injuries and emergencies

The telephone in the College pavilion, or any available mobile phone, may be used to summon assistance. The captain or team leader should ensure prior to the fixture that the approach road to the pavilion is clear for vehicular access.

If any person becomes ill or is injured (other than minor cuts, bruises etc.), arrangements should be made to accompany and transport him/her back to the College, or to the doctors surgery or hospital as appropriate. A taxi may be summoned through the College lodge for this purpose if necessary.

In cases of serious injury or illness, the ambulance service should be summoned by dialling 999, giving clear instructions as to the precise location of the incident, and providing a telephone contact number. Prior to the arrival of the emergency services, do not attempt to move a person who is immobilised by injury.

The senior tutor or tutorial office should be advised as soon as possible in case of any serious injury or emergency.

QUESTIONS AND TASKS

1. Read the case study outlining the procedures at this college and then produce a checklist of the procedures as an aid to easily understanding what is required in different cases.

    Answer ....

    ....

    ....

    ....

    ....

CHAPTER 2 – Health, safety and injury

RISK ASSESSMENT

CASE STUDY 2.15
SWIMMING POOL CHEMICAL FEARS

Scientists are calling for more research into the levels of chemicals added to swimming pool water after it was found they were significantly higher than in tap water. Earlier studies suggested the chemicals could harm unborn babies, and experts have moved to reassure pregnant women that swimming is safe. The most recent study calls for chlorination levels to be reduced as a precautionary measure. Many antenatal classes involve regular swimming sessions as this can provide much-needed exercise without overstressing the joints. Chemicals such as chlorine are added to pools in higher concentrations than in tap water in order to kill off potentially harmful bacteria. A survey tested the water from eight swimming pools in the London area and published the results in the journal *Occupational and Environmental Medicine*. The report concluded that levels of these by-products, called trihalomethanes, were much higher in pool water than in tap water.

Dust reaction is formed when chlorine comes into contact with organic material such as dust, sweat or skin. Chloroform, the most common trihalomethane, was measured at more than 20 times the level found in tap water. The Imperial College of Science and Technology in London said that earlier studies suggested that uptake of such chemicals could be as much as 141 times greater in a one-hour swim than in a 10-minute shower. Swimmers could be absorbing the chemicals through the skin, inhaling them as they evaporated, or swallowing water.

Nevertheless, other experts moved swiftly to reaffirm the safety of swimming. The chairman of the National Pool Water Treatment Advisory Group said that the chemicals were needed to protect swimmers from infections and that techniques had been refined over past decades. He added that the medical benefits of swimming far outweigh any problems caused by chemicals.

QUESTIONS AND TASKS

Visit the web site of the swimming pool operators and owners at www.caromal.co.uk/.
Find the resource pages with information for swimming pool engineers and pool owners and answer the following questions continuing on a separate sheet, if necessary:

1   What are their 14 suggestions for safe handling of swimming pool chemicals?

    Answer ....
    ....
    ....
    ....
    ....

2   What are the minimum personal protective equipment suggestions?

    Answer ....
    ....

RISK ASSESSMENT

CASE STUDY 2.16
FIELD EVENTS

Field events, especially throwing events, in athletics can, by their very nature, be dangerous unless they are carried out and supervised with care. There is no need for there to be any danger; this is borne out by the hundreds of thousands of throws and jumps that are made each year without mishap.

In practice, throwing events cannot be taught properly in class instruction except by way of preliminary demonstration. In general it is recommended that the size of groups to be coached should be limited to a number that can be controlled easily and effectively.

Throwing implements should be treated with respect at all times; they should not be played with or mishandled when carried from pavilion to playing field. Javelins should, if possible, be carried in portable storage stands that can be taken from the store onto the practice or competition areas. In no circumstances should a student run with a javelin except in the process of making a proper throw in practice or competition.

All throwers should stand well behind the circle or scratch line and remain there until one of them is told to move forward to make a throw. The discus and hammer should not be thrown where there is any other activity going on within throwing distance from the circle, and members awaiting their throws must stand well clear from the circle and away from the direction of the throw.

Particular care should be taken to see that when the grass is wet, the discus is dried before each throw. Attention is drawn to the value of a captive discus for coaching techniques in the preliminary stages of the event. In discus throwing a wide margin of error should be allowed for; a properly constructed safety net should be provided at the rear of the circle and checked at regular intervals.

Only one member should be allowed to throw at a time and both s/he and the organiser must make sure that there is no one in the general area of the intended line of flight of the implement before a throw is made. This responsibility should rest with the participant as well as the activity organiser.

It is important that the thrower shall remain behind the circle or scratch line after throwing; he must not immediately run after the implement. The implement must be retrieved only on instruction, and then it must be carried back in the correct way to the circle or scratch line. In no circumstances must it be thrown back.

In putting the shot, athletes must not be allowed to play about with the shot especially when other people are near. Care must also be taken when shots are being taken from or returned to store.

Protective cages are an essential protection for hammer throwing in competition, practice or coaching, but they are of little use unless they are firmly fixed to the ground. Preferably they should be constructed of metal, but fibre netting can be used.

Nets should be placed round the rear half of the discus circle. A safety net is recommended at the end of the discus sector, especially on wet grass when the discus slides and can be a danger.

Stop nets are now obtainable for coaching in a limited area or indoors.

Practice turns in the hammer event should only be allowed within the protective cage.

Throwing arcs should be clearly marked out by poles linked by rope to stop people wandering into them by accident.

The landing area for high jump should be no less than 5 metres × 3 metres and pole vault 6.5 metres × 5 metres.

If the edges of a landing area are lined with wood or concrete, this should be flush with the ground, and covered at places where a jumper is likely to hit it. A convenient or

continued →

CHAPTER 2 – Health, safety and injury

RISK ASSESSMENT

CASE STUDY 2.16 *continued*

adequate cover can be made of small sacks loosely filled with cork, granular chips or rubber scrap. In the pole vault the landing area should be built up to a height of 3 or 4 feet with rubber scrap.

The sand in the long- and triple-jump landing area should be sharp sand that will not cake and it should be deep enough to ensure that there will be no jar on landing. It should be dug over every few jumps with a fork or a spade; a rake is adequate only for levelling. It is important to see that these implements are not left lying on the ground with the teeth pointing upwards. It is also important to ensure that the sand is free from pieces of metal, wire or glass.

The instructor and the jumper must be careful to see that no jump is made while the landing area is being dug or raked.

Where the runway is of cinder or earth, constant attention is necessary to ensure that the surface is even and firm.

The long-jump take-off board must be of regulation dimensions and must be firmly fixed in the ground. This board should be painted white and kept clean at all times. A rocking board may cause serious damage to the instep. When a cinder runway becomes worn so that the edge of the take-off board is no longer level with the cinder, it should be repacked and rolled; but in the case of a grass runway the worn area should be dug out and replaced with a large thick sod which should be watered-in and rolled and left at least 24 hours before it is used.

It is always dangerous to have the take-off boards for the long jump and triple jump on the same runway. Different landing areas should be provided for each event.

When only one landing area can be provided, the runway should be wide enough for staggered boards and the landing area should be made wider.

QUESTIONS AND TASKS

1. Using this case study as a guide, visit your local athletics facility and compare the recommendations with the conditions at the facility. Produce a checklist to assist you in carrying out this task.

   Answer ....
   ....
   ....
   ....
   ....
   ....
   ....
   ....
   ....
   ....

CHAPTER 2 – Health, safety and injury

RISK ASSESSMENT

CASE STUDY 2.17
POLE VAULT AND HIGH-JUMP SOFT LANDING AREAS

Teachers and coaches of athletics should be aware of the real danger of serious and permanent injury which may result from the method of jumping known as the Fosbury Flop in which the athlete leaps backwards over the high-jump bar and lands on the upper part of his back.

For athletes using this technique the normal sandpit landing area is totally inadequate and dangerous. Practice of this technique by those who choose to employ it despite the inherent risks should be undertaken only at institutions and centres where proper built-up soft landing facilities and expert coaching are available.

Every endeavour must be made to provide suitable landing areas for high-jumpers and pole vaulters, but responsibility rests on the officials in these events to check that the landing area is safely prepared and suitable for them before competing.

The dimensions of soft landing areas are as follows:

- High jump: not less than 5 m long (that is, at the take-off side) by 4 m wide.
- Pole vault: not less than 5 m × 5 m.

Only landing areas manufactured by well-known and established firms should be used, and these must be checked regularly to see that they conform to standard.

QUESTIONS AND TASKS

1. Using this case study as a guide, visit your local athletics facility and compare the recommendations with the conditions at the facility. Produce a checklist to assist you in carrying out this task.

   Answer ....

CHAPTER 2 – Health, safety and injury

RISK ASSESSMENT

CASE STUDY 2.18
COMPETITION

In competition, in order to avoid accidents, sectors should be roped off. The ropes should be of such height that they cannot be casually stepped over. The ropes should be well away from the sector lines marked on the ground for each event as designated in the British Athletics Federation rulebook.

Instruction must be given that implements must be thrown only from the circles or scratch line or the immediate vicinity thereof, that they must be returned by hand during practice or competition, and that they must not be thrown back to the starting area.

Besides the roping off, it is important to have permanent notices displayed outside the ropes to warn spectators who may unthinkingly step over or under the ropes.

It is important to site the circles and scratch lines so that there is no likelihood of the implement landing among spectators, or judges or competitors in other events, either in fair throw or if an implement slips out of the competitor's hand.

Definite instructions must be given as to who (competitor or steward) is to retrieve and return the implement. It must never be thrown back.

One of the judges of field events should, between trials (while the jump or throw is being measured), stand in the circle, on the scratch line, or in front of the take-off board, in order to make sure that the next competitor does not take his trial until all is clear.

Spectators and other competitors must be kept well away and out of the danger area when a competitor is throwing.

A loudhailer or some other form of audible warning is of great value to judges of field events.

In general, as there is inevitably a good deal of waiting or standing around during both instruction and competition in field events, it is advisable to stress the importance of keeping the body warm. Poor performances and pulled muscles often result from cold bodies. If a competitor does not have a tracksuit he should wear a sweater, anorak or overcoat and a pair of flannel trousers. This is recommended on warm days and is of vital importance on cold days.

Athletes should be encouraged to warm up for all events both before practice and before competition.

Every care must be exercised in the layout of grounds and training areas, especially where two or more throwing areas are positioned close to each other. It is essential to ensure that the areas are planned and positioned so that there are no danger zones as far as competitors or officials and spectators are concerned.

The positions of the throwing areas on many tracks are dangerous and some discus and hammer circles are so badly positioned that the discus or hammer can, on occasions, land on the running track. At the larger athletic meetings and tracks where concentrated training takes place, a separate field-event practice area should be provided.

QUESTIONS AND TASKS

1. Using this case study as a guide, visit your local athletics facility during a competition and compare the recommendations with the conditions at the facility. Produce a checklist to assist you in carrying out this task. Continue your answer on a separate sheet.

   Answer ....
   ....

CHAPTER 2 – Health, safety and injury

RISK ASSESSMENT

CASE STUDY 2.19
TRACK EVENTS

Great responsibility and control are necessary to prevent accidents caused by spikes.

Careful instruction as to care and safety precautions should be given at the earliest opportunity.

All races of one lap or less should be run in lanes and it is particularly important that during the changeover in relay races this rule should be enforced.

In races of more than one lap, the start should be as far away from a bend as possible to avoid bunching and jockeying for position.

When spikes are worn, numbers in events should be limited, for example to eight in the 800 metres, and the maximum numbers recommended for events should not be exceeded.

The tape at the finish is not a tape but a length of worsted that should break easily. It should be adjusted for height so that there is no risk of its searing the necks of competitors.

Hurdles should not have loose top bars. They should be rigidly constructed, with a smooth, rounded finish, free from the danger of sharp or protruding edges and they must be of the correct weight and resistance.

QUESTIONS AND TASKS

1   Using this case study as a guide, visit your local athletics facility and compare the recommendations with the conditions at the facility. Produce a checklist to assist you in carrying out this task.

    Answer ....

CHAPTER 2 – Health, safety and injury

RISK ASSESSMENT

CASE STUDY 2.20
MEMBERS' RESPONSIBILITIES

The previous case studies have attempted to highlight some of the risks associated with athletics and to suggest how control measures may be put in place. Below is a copy of a risk assessment form completed by an athletics club committee. Everyone has a responsibility for safety to some extent. Members of athletics clubs are responsible for reporting any dangerous occurrences or accidents they are made aware of so that these are included in the following year's risk assessment. Similarly members are responsible for making the club committee aware of any medical conditions that may affect their abilities in the sport.

Risk Assessment Form
Club: *Athletics*
Date: *01/10/04*
Please list the types of activity your club undertakes both during practice sessions and when competing:
Running (synthetic indoor and outdoor tracks)
Hurdles
High Jump
Long jump/triple jump
Shot-put
Circuit training (sit-ups, push-ups, squat-thrusts, etc.)

Identified hazard
Running

Risks involved
Muscle strains/pulls

Control measures
Thorough warm-up (jogging, stretching, etc.)
In consideration of the above, how would you evaluate the level of risk arising from this activity?
Low

Identified hazard
High jump/hurdles

Risks involved
Collision with equipment

Control measures
Training supervised by members experienced at event.
In consideration of the above, how would you evaluate the level of risk arising from this activity?
Low

QUESTIONS AND TASKS

1. Using the information from this case study, in particular how the various risks have been assessed, prepare a similar risk assessment for three other sports activities of your choice. Write your answer on a separate sheet.

IVA REVISION AND PREPARATION

Students will need to do the following to meet the grading criteria of this unit:

- Choose FOUR different sports situations and prepare a list of injury and risk factors for each situation.
- Prepare a list of ways in which the injuries can be minimised.
- Draw up a list of common sports injuries and how they are treated (by the athlete and the specialist).
- Prepare a checklist for TWO different sports injuries that aims to assess the severity of the injury.
- Carry out a practical risk assessment of a sports activity, taking into account laws, rules and regulations.

ANSWERS AND GUIDELINES TO CASE STUDY 2.1

1. The average weight of a jockey is 45 kilograms (100 pounds)
2. Simply increasing the weight limits for jockeys would prevent them having to lose so much weight. A useful primer on this can be found at www.10news.com/investigations/3653385/detail.html.

ANSWERS AND GUIDELINES TO CASE STUDY 2.2

QPR were the first British club to install an artificial playing pitch in 1981, followed by Luton in 1985, Oldham and Preston in 1986. It was one of football's 'bright ideas' that did not last. QPR went back to grass in 1988, Oldham and Luton in 1991 (when the pitches were banned in Division 1) and Preston in 1994.

Good sources for these tasks include the following:

- www.manutdsoccerschools.com/index.html
- www.footballculture.net/players
- www.fifa.com/en/development/pitch/index/

ANSWERS AND GUIDELINES TO CASE STUDY 2.3

1. The Belfast-born fighter was granted his licence in June 2002 after the British Boxing Board of Control had assessed neurological reports to satisfy them that he was fit to box. The former world champion had been battling with the British Board to get permission to box again in Britain following the detection of a cyst near his brain in November 2000.

   He had been cleared in the US and made a winning return to the ring earlier in the year having been licensed by the Nevada State Athletic Commission.

ANSWERS AND GUIDELINES TO CASE STUDY 2.4

A very good summary of the SARS (Severe Acute Respiratory Syndrome) epidemic and the spread of the virus can be found at http://news.bbc.co.uk/1/hi/worldservice/specials/171sars_story/index.shtml

ANSWERS AND GUIDELINES TO CASE STUDY 2.5

1. For the implications to Schumacher's season see www.formula1.com/news/1844.html.
2. In an extreme case such as this, vertebroplasty may be the only option. It is a procedure that allows the doctor to inject a glue-like material, through a needle, into and around the vertebrae.

ANSWERS AND GUIDELINES TO CASE STUDY 2.6

1. For a full explanation of the injury and its treatments see www.spine-inc.com/glossary/p/prolapsed-disc.html and www.patient.co.uk/showdoc/21692509/.
2. An update on Ben Blair's fortunes can be found at http://news.bbc.co.uk/sport1/hi/rugby_union/rugby_world_cup/team_pages/new_zealand/3199878.stm.

ANSWERS AND GUIDELINES TO CASE STUDY 2.7

1. Common rugby injuries include the following:
   - concussion – the most common head injury in sport. It is caused by a temporary disturbance in brain function due to trauma;
   - shoulder injuries such as bruising, sprains and strains are very common in collision sports;
   - hamstrings form the group of muscles at the back of the thigh. A hamstring strain is caused by an over-stretch, tear, or complete rupture of one or more of the three hamstring muscles;

- knee strain – a stretch, tear, or complete rupture of one or more of the knee ligaments;
- ankle sprain – an overstretching or tearing of one or more ankle ligaments. Ankle injuries are the most frequent injuries in rugby.

2   It would normally take up to 12 months to recover fully. For more information see: http://news.bbc.co.uk/sport1/hi/rugby_union/international/3975111.stm.

ANSWERS AND GUIDELINES TO CASE STUDY 2.8

1   Dehydration occurs when the body does not have as much water and fluids as it should. Dehydration can be caused by losing too much fluid, not drinking enough water or fluids, or both. Vomiting and diarrhoea are common causes. Infants and children are more susceptible to dehydration than adults because of their smaller body weights and higher turnover of water and electrolytes. The elderly and the sick are also at higher risk.

Dehydration is classified as mild, moderate, or severe according to how much of the body's fluid is lost or not replenished. When severe, dehydration is a life-threatening emergency.

Dehydration impairs both physical and mental performance. A change in body weight of 1 kg corresponds to a loss of 1 litre of fluid through sweat. A loss of 2 per cent in body weight through sweating causes an increase in perceived effort and is claimed to reduce performance by 10–20 per cent. A 3–5 per cent loss noticeably reduces aerobic performance and impairs reaction time, judgement, concentration and decision making.

2   The average adult needs to consume approximately 2.5 litres of water per day. If exercising then obviously a lot more water is needed. Maintaining adequate fluid and carbohydrate (CHO) intake is the key to staying hydrated and being able to train or race longer and harder. There are many sports drinks on the market that do both these jobs.

Water is always stated as the optimal drink for endurance exercise but alone it causes bloating and stimulates urine output, therefore it is inefficiently retained. Sports drinks have the benefit of including sodium (salt), which helps speed fluid absorption, and CHO which provides fuel. The amount of fluid versus CHO required depends on the physiological demands of the sport and the climate conditions. If sweat rates are high and dehydration is rapid then fluid replacement should take priority.

ANSWERS AND GUIDELINES TO CASE STUDY 2.9

1   The reasons behind Paula Radcliffe's failures at the Olympics are still unclear. Insights can be found at:
- http://news.bbc.co.uk/sport2/hi/olympics_2004/3590166.stm
- http://news.bbc.co.uk/sport1/hi/olympics_2004/athletics/3589132.stm
- www2.real-berlin-marathon.com/world/E/news/show/002582.

2   Paula Radcliffe suffered more Olympic agony when she dropped out of the 10,000 m final with eight laps remaining.

ANSWERS AND GUIDELINES TO CASE STUDY 2.10

1   A sudden sharp pain in the calf muscle followed by difficulty using it usually indicates a calf strain. The most common place to get this injury is at the tendon junction of the gastrocnemius roughly half way between the knee and the heel. Contracting the muscle against resistance with the legs straight can test this. Pain is felt midway up the calf muscle.

If Brian has damaged the soleus muscle he might get pain lower in the leg and also pain when he contracts the muscle against resistance with the knee bent. The gastrocnemius muscle originates above the knee and inserts via the Achilles tendon to the heel. The soleus originates below the knee and also inserts via the Achilles tendon.

2   What can the athlete do?
- rest, ice, compression, elevation are essential
- see a sports injury professional who can advise on treatment and rehabilitation
- wear a heel pad to raise the heel and shorten the calf muscle hence taking some of the strain off it.

What could a sports injury specialist do?
- prescribe anti-inflammatory medication, e.g. ibuprofen, which is beneficial in the first few days after the injury
- use ultrasound treatment
- use a compression device
- use sports massage techniques after the initial acute phase
- prescribe a full rehabilitation programme.

ANSWERS AND GUIDELINES TO CASE STUDY 2.11

1. She probably has a sprained finger. This is caused when the finger is bent in some way causing damage to the ligaments that connect the bones. It is common in ball games such as American football, basketball, cricket, handball and so on. The ligaments at the side of the finger (collateral ligaments) are often damaged.

2. What can the athlete do?
   - rest the finger and apply ice. Ice massage with a single ice cube may be suitable
   - tape the finger to protect it while it is healing.

   What can the sports injury professional do?
   - advise on rehabilitation
   - tape the finger for support
   - operate if required, for example on a complete rupture.

ANSWERS AND GUIDELINES TO CASE STUDY 2.12

A hamstring strain, or a pulled hamstring as it is sometimes called, is a tear in one of the hamstring muscles (semitendinosis, semimembrinosis and biceps femoris). It often results from an overload of the muscles or trying to move the muscles too fast.

Strains are common in all sports especially those that involve sprinting. Running injuries to the hamstring are very common. They range from a complete rupture of the muscle to small micro-tears that the athlete will probably not notice at the time.

Symptoms include:
- a sudden sharp pain at the back of the leg
- muscles going into spasm
- swelling and bruising.

If the rupture is very bad it may be possible to feel a gap in the muscle.

Strains are graded 1, 2 or 3 depending on severity. A grade 1 might consist of small micro-tears in the muscle. A grade 2 would be a partial tear in the muscle, and grade 3 is a severe or complete rupture of the muscle.

1. Grade 1 – what can the athlete do?
   - use a compression bandage or heat retainer until no pain is felt
   - see a sports injury professional who can advise on rehabilitation and strengthening.

   Grade 1 – what can a sports injury specialist or doctor do?
   - Use sports massage techniques to speed up recovery
   - use ultrasound and electrical stimulation
   - prescribe a rehabilitation programme.

   Grade 2 – what can the athlete do?
   - ice, compress, elevate, use crutches for three to five days
   - see a sports injury specialist who can advise on rehabilitation.

   Grade 2 – what can a sports injury specialist or doctor do?
   - use sports massage techniques to speed up recovery
   - use ultrasound and electrical stimulation
   - prescribe a rehabilitation programme including stretching and strengthening exercises.

   Grade 3 – what can the athlete do?
   - seek medical attention immediately
   - rest, ice, compress, elevate
   - use crutches
   - see a sports injury professional who can advise on rehabilitation and prevention.

   Grade 3 – what can a sports injury specialist or doctor do?
   - use sports massage techniques to speed up recovery
   - use ultrasound and electrical stimulation
   - prescribe a rehabilitation programme and monitor it
   - operate if necessary.

2. The athlete is likely to be on crutches for 4–6 weeks.

ANSWERS AND GUIDELINES TO CASE STUDY 2.13

1. Acupuncture is a branch of traditional Chinese medicine which also includes herbal medicine, massage techniques, exercise therapies, nutritional therapy and spiritual healing. Fine, sterile needles are gently inserted into selected points on the skin, known as acupoints. This is said to balance the flow of vital energy (Qi, pronounced 'chee') in the body and regulate the function of the inner organs. Acupuncture is used to treat a wide range of common ailments and also for pain relief and to promote general health. It is one of the most widely

used and researched forms of complementary therapy.

2. Endorphins are neurohormone polypeptide molecules, synthesised by the hypothalamus of the brain and secreted into the bloodstream by the pituitary gland. There are four different types of endorphin produced in the body: Alpha, Beta, Gamma and Sigma. Beta endorphins consist of 30 amino acid sub-units and it is the beta endorphins that show the greatest increase in plasma concentration during exercise. Endorphins are released from the pituitary during times of pain or stress. Studies have looked into the affect of acidosis (caused by exercise) on endorphin release. Exercise-induced acidosis of the blood takes place when prolonged exercise has occurred and oxygen flow to the muscles has decreased. Anaerobic respiration occurs causing lactic acid accumulation, which results in acidosis. This acidosis is then thought to stimulate the pituitary to release the endorphins.

3. Kirlian photography is different from normal photography. The Kirlian camera has a plate (rather than a lens), which is charged by a high-frequency coil, and can only photograph objects in immediate contact with it. The photograph, therefore, must be taken in the darkroom. The photosensitive paper is placed directly onto the machine and the hands (or whatever is being photographed) are then placed, one at a time, onto the paper while the machine is energised for a few seconds. The paper is developed in the normal way. The picture is an interference pattern between two fields of energy: the energy generated by the camera and that generated by the human aura. Studies have shown that the corona emanation does not relate to skin temperature, resistance or to perspiration. This process, discovered by Semyon and Valentina Kirlian in 1939, has since been extensively researched and refined by independent laboratories and health practitioners around the world, being used in the material sciences, biological sciences, agriculture, pharmaceutical research and holistic health. Any other aura camera which does not use this same process is not, technically, a Kirlian camera.

ANSWERS AND GUIDELINES TO CASE STUDY 2.14

1. Students should be encouraged to itemise the details in the case study and perhaps present the material in the form of a flow chart.

ANSWERS AND GUIDELINES TO CASE STUDY 2.15

Handling safety points:

1. ALWAYS wear a good pair of chemical-proof rubber gloves when handling any chemicals.
2. ALWAYS wear splash-proof goggles when handling exposed chemicals.
3. ALWAYS wear a good-quality dust mask when handling powdered chemicals.
4. ALWAYS wear the correct respirator if handling chemicals that may fume or gas.
5. ALWAYS wear a suitable protective apron to keep splashes and chemical dust off your clothes.
6. ALWAYS ensure all children and other people are well away from you when you are handling or dosing chemicals.
7. ALWAYS wash your hands after handling chemicals or chemical containers.
8. ALWAYS allow at least 15 minutes for the chemicals to disperse before allowing anyone into the water.
9. ALWAYS stand upwind if you have to throw chlorine granules directly into the pool.
10. NEVER allow pool chemicals to come into contact with your skin.
11. NEVER wear absorbent shoes e.g. trainers when handling liquid chemicals.
12. NEVER wear trousers tucked INSIDE rubber boots – particularly if handling liquid chemicals.
13. NEVER smoke, eat or drink when handling or dosing chemicals.
14. NEVER add chemicals to a pool while anyone is in the water.

The following is considered the minimum personal protective equipment (PPE) equipment in the UK:

- an eyewash station adjacent to each main chemical handling or decanting point
- a respirator capable of dealing with acid and chlorine gases and vapours
- chemical splash-proof eye protection (ordinary spectacles are no protection)
- chemical-resistant gloves or gauntlets
- chemical-resistant apron
- chemical-resistant and waterproof boots.

Additional PPE is also recommended on the Health and Safety Executive web site at www.hse.gov.uk/pubns/.

ANSWERS AND GUIDELINES TO CASE STUDY 2.16

1. Students should prepare for a visit to a local athletics facility by creating a simple checklist of the factors included in the case study. A useful addition to this activity would be a short interview with the safety officer at the facility. This activity is continued in Case Study 2.17.

ANSWERS AND GUIDELINES TO CASE STUDY 2.17

1. Students should prepare for a visit to a local athletics facility by creating a simple checklist of the factors included in the case study. A useful addition to this activity would be a short interview with the safety officer at the facility. This activity is continued in Case Study 2.18.

ANSWERS AND GUIDELINES TO CASE STUDY 2.18

1. Students should prepare for a visit to a local athletics facility during a competition by creating a simple checklist of the factors included in the case study. A useful addition to this activity would be a short interview with the safety officer at the facility. This activity is continued in the next case study.

ANSWERS AND GUIDELINES TO CASE STUDY 2.19

1. Students should prepare for a visit to a local athletics facility by creating a simple checklist of the factors included in the case study. A useful addition to this activity would be a short interview with the safety officer at the facility. This activity is continued in this next case study.

ANSWERS AND GUIDELINES TO CASE STUDY 2.20

1. Students should be encouraged to think of the risk assessments related to one of their own common sports activities. They should use the same format for risk assessment as contained in the case study.

CHAPTER 3: Preparation for sport

The information on this page is intended to help you plan and deliver your lessons using BTEC First Sport *by John Honeybourne.*

OVERVIEW

This chapter looks at the essential preparation required for successful sports performances. The chapter investigates fitness levels required and lifestyle choices necessary for a participant and how to carry out basic field tests on fitness.

Fitness training regimes are investigated, together with institutional requirements and psychological preparations. The primary goals of the chapter are:

- to look at fitness levels and lifestyle of an individual in a particular sport
- to plan a simple fitness training programme
- to look at the nutritional requirements of sports participants
- to look at how psychological factors affect training and performance.

ADVICE AND GUIDANCE TO STUDENTS

This chapter covers the theory and the practice related to sports fitness, nutrition and psychology. Once students have covered the theory they will be able to put some of the concepts into practice by designing sports fitness tests and a two-week training programme. They will also be able to prepare dietary guidelines and look at the psychological factors that affect training and performance. In order to understand the demands of the IVA, it is useful to appreciate exactly what the tutor will be looking for. A detailed view of this is shown in the following table:

PASS	To obtain a MERIT do this as well	To obtain a DISTINCTION do this as well
Contrast the fitness and lifestyle of two sports performers and comment on the effect of this on performance.	Identify and define the fitness and lifestyle issues which affect performance.	Evaluate the factors and provide recommendations for improvement.
Using teacher support, conduct and record a suitable fitness test to assess fitness levels.	Do this independently and comment on the results.	Critically analyse the results of the tests, draw conclusions and make recommendations.
Using teacher support, plan a two-week training programme.	Do this independently.	Evaluate the programme and make medium- and long-term recommendations.
Prepare and present dietary guidance for two selected athletes.	Explain dietary guidance and meal plans.	Compare the two guidelines and draw conclusions.
Identify basic psychological factors affecting training and performance.	Describe the psychological factors.	Critically analyse the factors and how they affect performance in the short and medium term.

CHAPTER 3 – Preparation for sport

SUGGESTED LESSON PLAN

TOPIC	HOURS	ACTIVITY TO USE	PAGE
Fitness level and lifestyle			
Physical fitness	5	Case Study 3.1 Physical fitness in football	63
Fitness levels	7	Case Study 3.2 Grip dynamometer	64
	5	Case Study 3.3 Body mass index	65
Fitness training programmes			
Fitness training methods	7	Case Study 3.4 Scottish plyometric training	66
		Case Study 3.5 Fartlek training	67
		Case Study 3.6 Interval training	68
Principles of training	3	Case Study 3.7 FITT principles – recent research	69
Fitness tests	3	Worksheet 1 Fitness tests	70
Nutritional requirements			
Nutrients	2	Case Study 3.8 England Rugby Team	72
Healthy diet	2	Case Study 3.9 US research	73
Nutrition strategies	2	Case Study 3.10 Sports drinks boost Olympic athletes	74
Different sports needs	2	Case Study 3.11 UK teacher wins California to New York marathon	75
Nutritional supplements	2		
Fitness testing	2	Case Study 3.12 Golf fitness	76
Psychological factors			
Motivation	2	Worksheet 2 Youth sports motivation questionnaire	77
Arousal and anxiety	2	Worksheet 3 Inverted U theory diagram	79
Personality tests	4	Worksheet 4 Questionnaire: Personality tests	80
Concentration	3	Case Study 3.13 Marat Safin	81
IVA revision and preparation	7		82

ANSWERS TO PROGRESS CHECK (PAGE 87, BTEC FIRST SPORT)

1 Name the main components of fitness.

Answer
The main components are:
- strength
- muscular and aerobic endurance
- flexibility
- power
- speed
- body composition.

Other components could include:
- agility
- co-ordination
- balance
- reaction time.

2 Choose two components and describe how you would test the level of fitness for each.

Answer
A strength test, for example, could involve the use of a handgrip dynamometer. A speed test could be measured by a 30 m sprint on a flat, non-slippery surface.

3 Explain how lifestyle factors can affect physical fitness.

Answer
Lifestyle factors can affect physical fitness in the following ways:
- They may influence stress levels.
- Participants may consume alcohol, cigarettes or drugs.
- Poor sleeping habits affect recovery rates.

4   Give the five main principles of training.

Answer

The five main principles of training are:

- specificity
- overload
- progression
- reversibility
- variance.

5   What is meant by the interval training method?

Answer

This is one of the most popular types of training, aimed at improving both aerobic and anaerobic fitness. It is known as interval training because it has periods of exercise and rest.

6   What are plyometrics?

Answer

Plyometrics are designed to improve dynamic strength. They improve the speed in which muscles shorten. Typically plyometric training involves bounding, hopping and jumping.

7   Why is the intake of water so crucial in sport?

Answer

The intake of water in sport is crucial because water is lost through sweat, and excessive loss of water can cause dehydration. The loss of water also leads to the loss of salt, which leads to cramp.

8   What is meant by a healthy diet?

Answer

A healthy diet means having a balanced intake of starch, including plenty of vegetables, salad and fruit, while keeping fat content to a minimum.

9   Give an example of intrinsic and extrinsic motivation – give sports examples for each.

Answer

Intrinsic motivation is an individual's internal drive, which helps them to perform well in sport. This means that the participant should enjoy and be satisfied by their involvement.

Extrinsic motivation is the external influences on the participant, such as the gain of rewards or praise and encouragement.

10   Using examples from sport, explain the inverted U hypothesis.

Answer

The inverted U hypothesis suggests that as arousal increases, so does performance, but only up to the point where a moderate arousal level has been reached. After this point and before it, performance is poor. An example from sport could be a well-motivated and driven participant, who is able to remain calm and concentrate on their skills in order to perform. Arousal levels at a moderate level mean that this participant performs well.

CHAPTER 3 – Preparation for sport

FITNESS LEVEL AND LIFESTYLE

CASE STUDY 3.1
PHYSICAL FITNESS IN FOOTBALL

Football is a multiple-sprint sport requiring players to spend some of their time sprinting, and the rest of the time running fast or slowly, walking or even standing still. Varying degrees of fitness are required depending on the player's position in the team, the amount of time spent on the field and the level at which the game is played. A full 90-minute match demands a high level of aerobic fitness.

The nature of the game means that energy demands are sometimes extremely high and sometimes fairly low. Studies have shown that at professional levels the average work-rate of midfield players and strikers is similar to that of a good marathon runner.

This means football players must have good aerobic endurance if they are to last the full game without becoming excessively tired. Because the game involves acceleration and deceleration, changes in direction, angled runs and running backwards there is also an increased energy need.

The fitness demands of the game depend largely on the level of competition and on the position of the player within the field.

A study looking at the ground distance covered by professional football players playing in different positions estimated that goalkeepers cover about 4000 metres during a game, whereas midfielders cover about 10,000 metres in the same time.

In addition, the sudden increase in speed as a player sprints for the ball taxes the anaerobic energy systems, that is, those energy systems that work without oxygen. Using these energy systems is very tiring and a quick recovery from this is important to the outcome of the game.

To play football well, the player should continue to participate throughout the year and/or train in the off-season as well as during the season. Running ability is important and cardiovascular fitness is best maintained with running activities.

QUESTIONS AND TASKS

1 What does the term 'aerobic endurance' mean?

   Answer ....
   ....
   ....
   ....

2 Suggest suitable drinks and food for footballers in order for them to obtain the kind of energy needed to play.

   Answer ....
   ....
   ....
   ....

CASE STUDY 3.2
GRIP DYNAMOMETER

A grip dynamometer is often used to test strength as it measures the force generated by the subject's grip in one hand. The test is carried out as follows:

- The grip dynamometer is adjusted to the correct size for the subject's hand.
- The subject grips the dynamometer with their dominant hand and raises the arm away from the body until the arm is level with their shoulder.
- The subject then slowly brings the arm down toward the body while applying maximum force to the grip dynamometer.
- The test ends as the hand reaches the subject's leg. Note: neither the subject's hand nor the grip dynamometer must touch the subject's leg or the side of their body.
- The subject gets three goes and the best one counts.
- The result is invalid if the subject's hand or the dynamometer touches the subject's leg or side.
- The subject must carry out an appropriate cool-down.
- Ensure that the subject feels all right and that you are happy for them to go.

The result can be compared with norms or previous tests.

QUESTIONS AND TASKS

1   As a group, carry out the grip dynamometer test. Having collected all of the data, take the following into account:
    - The gender of individuals in the group.
    - The age of individuals in the group.
    - The weight of individuals in the group.

FITNESS LEVEL AND LIFESTYLE

CASE STUDY 3.3
BODY MASS INDEX

The most common benchmark of healthy weight for adults is based on height and weight and is called body mass index (BMI).

BMI is a good indicator of the total amount of body fat and is a reliable predictor of the likelihood of disease associated with being too heavy (or too light).

BMI is calculated with the formula:

$$\left[BMI = \frac{\text{weight (in kg)}}{\text{height (in metres)}} \right]$$

To work out your BMI, divide your weight in kilograms by your height in metres, and then divide that figure by your height again.

Understanding your BMI

Underweight – BMI less than 18.5
Some people in the underweight category (BMI under 18.5) are naturally lean and healthy. But being underweight can also be bad for your health. If you are in the underweight category and have been restricting your diet, you should aim to gain weight and get back into the normal weight range for your height. If you are finding it difficult to put on weight, or you lose a lot of weight rapidly, you should see your doctor.

Healthy weight – BMI 18.5–24.9
If you are in the normal category (BMI 18.5–24.9) for your weight and height, you should aim to maintain your weight through a combination of healthy diet and physical activity. Do not be tempted to try to get into the underweight category.

Overweight – BMI 25.0–29.9
If you are in the overweight category (BMI 25–29.9) you should concentrate on not gaining any more weight. Try to cut down on sugary and fatty foods and on the amount you eat in order to get back into the normal weight range for your height. Increasing your levels of physical activity will help.

Obese – BMI 30.0–39.9
If your body mass index is obese (BMI 30–39.9) or morbidly obese (BMI over 40) then your risk of health problems is high. It is important that you try to lose some weight and you should consider asking for help from your doctor.

QUESTIONS AND TASKS

1   Test your own BMI and then suggest the limitations of BMI.

    Answer ....
    ....
    ....
    ....
    ....

FITNESS TRAINING PROGRAMMES

CASE STUDY 3.4
SCOTTISH PLYOMETRIC TRAINING

Motherwell's head of youth development, Chris McCart, is optimistic that Scotland is set for fame in football by 2010. Claiming that a revolution has occurred in youth football in Scotland over the last five years, McCart says that young players are being coached three or four times a week by many Scottish clubs, saying 'these boys are exposed to sports science programmes, specialised coaching sessions, fitness techniques like plyometrics, as well as work on developing fast feet.'

Celtic are investing £1.5 million a year in youth development and are already seeing the benefits. McCart believes that Scottish football's financial situation will result in further development of young players as clubs choose Scottish players rather than buying expensive players from abroad.

QUESTIONS AND TASKS

1 What are plyometrics?

   Answer ....

2 Identify the key points to consider before starting plyometrics training.

   Answer ....

CASE STUDY 3.5
FARTLEK TRAINING

Fartlek training is a Swedish name for speed play. It involves changing the pace during the athlete's running, from anaerobic to aerobic running.

A typical session would be:

- easy running: four minutes
- half-pace running: four minutes
- easy running: four minutes
- series of 6 × 100 m sprints with easy running between sprints
- easy running: two minutes
- series of 6 × 50 m hill sprints with easy running between sprints
- warm-down easy running: two minutes.

QUESTIONS AND TASKS

1 The case study outlines the basic fartlek techniques. What are the different types of fartlek training and what kind of sports activities are they designed for?

   Answer ....
   ....
   ....
   ....
   ....
   ....
   ....
   ....
   ....
   ....
   ....
   ....

CHAPTER 3 – Preparation for sport

FITNESS TRAINING PROGRAMMES

CASE STUDY 3.6
INTERVAL TRAINING

Interval training involves periods of hard work followed by a timed period of rest, repeated several times in one training session.

The periods of hard work are called high-intensity activity.

An example of interval training is 10 fast runs over 40 metres, with a two-minute rest between each run.

Distance, speed and the length of recovery time can be varied to suit the level of fitness and the sport.

Interval training develops both aerobic and anaerobic fitness.

QUESTIONS AND TASKS

1 What is the basic purpose of interval training?

   Answer ....

   ....

   ....

   ....

   ....

   ....

   ....

   ....

   ....

   ....

2 What are the rules to be considered before starting interval training?

   Answer ....

   ....

   ....

   ....

   ....

   ....

   ....

   ....

   ....

   ....

FITNESS TRAINING PROGRAMMES

CASE STUDY 3.7
FITT PRINCIPLES – RECENT RESEARCH

It has been claimed that regular exercise is the closest thing we have in this world to an anti-aging drug and that it is never too late to start or to reap the benefits.

A recent research study of inactive elderly men who took up regular exercise found tremendous gains in strength and cardiovascular fitness, which resulted in less disease, less aches and pains, greater energy, and better over-all emotional and physical health. The physiological benefits of exercise are the enhancement of practically every organ, system, and cell leading to decreased risk of almost every lifestyle-related health problem, as well as weight control or loss. A recent review of research showed that exercise also significantly improves mood and well-being, reduces anxiety, depression and stress, improves self-concept, self-esteem and self-assurance, and even improves creativity. Physiologists have found that as little as 10 minutes a day can yield positive benefits.

QUESTIONS AND TASKS

1. What is the basic recommendation to begin FITT training?

   Answer ....
   ....
   ....

2. Which training exercises do you recommend for cardiovascular fitness?

   Answer ....
   ....
   ....

3. Which training exercises do you recommend for muscular strength improvement?

   Answer ....
   ....
   ....

CHAPTER 3 – Preparation for sport

WORKSHEET 1 FITNESS TRAINING PROGRAMMES: FITNESS TESTS

Name: ....   Event: ....

Location: ....   Height/Distance/Time: ....

Date: ....   Position: ....

Did you achieve your performance goal?   Yes ☐   No ☐   Partly ☐

> What was your performance goal? (e.g. improve PB, quality for next round)

Did you achieve your process goal?   Yes ☐   No ☐   Partly ☐

> What was your process goal? (e.g. explosive start, elbow drive)

Were you or did you have:

completely determined to achieve performance goal?	Yes ☐	No ☐	Partly ☐
completely determined to achieve process goal?	Yes ☐	No ☐	Partly ☐
highly physically activated?	Yes ☐	No ☐	Partly ☐
no worries or fears?	Yes ☐	No ☐	Partly ☐
in complete control?	Yes ☐	No ☐	Partly ☐
mentally calm?	Yes ☐	No ☐	Partly ☐
complete task focus?	Yes ☐	No ☐	Partly ☐
complete commitment to fully extend yourself?	Yes ☐	No ☐	Partly ☐
complete confidence in physical preparation?	Yes ☐	No ☐	Partly ☐
complete confidence in mental preparation?	Yes ☐	No ☐	Partly ☐
complete confidence in abilities to achieve goal?	Yes ☐	No ☐	Partly ☐
willing to take necessary risks?	Yes ☐	No ☐	Partly ☐
did you follow a race preparation plan?	Yes ☐	No ☐	Partly ☐

> If partly, which parts were NOT followed and why?

Rate the effectiveness of:

general physical warm-up preparation	Good ☐	Average ☐	Bad ☐
event-specific physical preparation	Good ☐	Average ☐	Bad ☐
relaxation	Good ☐	Average ☐	Bad ☐
mental preparation	Good ☐	Average ☐	Bad ☐
warm down	Good ☐	Average ☐	Bad ☐
event review	Good ☐	Average ☐	Bad ☐

During the event did your focus of attention stay on your event focus plan?   Yes ☐   No ☐

> When you were going well, where was your focus?

WORKSHEET I (CONTINUED) FITNESS TRAINING PROGRAMMES: FITNESS TESTS

When you were going less well, where was your focus?

Did anything unexpected happen that impacted your performance (for better or worse)?   Yes ☐   No ☐

Give details:

Should anything be changed or adapted for the next competition?   Yes ☐   No ☐

Give details:

QUESTIONS AND GUIDELINES

1   Complete the above form for a sporting activity.

2   What does the form say about your overall fitness and preparation for the activity?

Answer ....

....

....

....

NUTRITIONAL REQUIREMENTS

CASE STUDY 3.8
ENGLAND RUGBY TEAM

England's rugby players are among the fittest sportsmen in the country thanks to their fitness adviser. The most noticeable difference is the size and the speed and strength of the players compared with those of up to 10 years ago. It is estimated that the average England back-row players now carry 10 kg more weight despite the fact that their body-fat levels have fallen by 5–10 per cent. This is due to a change in diet. The approach has been a high protein but moderate carbohydrate diet. Less sugary food and more organic, unrefined sources of carbohydrate are encouraged. White bread, white pasta and other refined sources of carbohydrate are taboo and unrefined sources like brown rice and sweet potatoes are the alternatives. A rise in blood sugar levels, the build up of muscle and faster recovery from injuries are the consequences. Lean sources of protein, such as chicken and oily fish, are also an important part of the diet.

QUESTIONS AND TASKS

1. What is the importance of proteins in the diet?

    Answer ....

    ....

    ....

    ....

    ....

    ....

    ....

2. What is the importance of carbohydrates in the diet?

    Answer ....

    ....

    ....

    ....

    ....

    ....

    ....

NUTRITIONAL REQUIREMENTS

CASE STUDY 3.9
US RESEARCH

A national telephone survey of a random sample of 2991 adults aged 16 and over provided detailed information from 1142 vitamin and mineral supplement users about their nutrient intake patterns from dietary supplements. Dietary supplement users were divided into four groups (light, moderate, heavy, and very heavy) on the basis of the type and amount of nutrient intake from supplements. The light, moderate, heavy, and very heavy nutrient intake groups accounted for 42 per cent, 16 per cent, 28 per cent, and 14 per cent, respectively, of the total users. Young supplement users (aged 16 to 25) tended to be in the light user group. Older adults (aged 41 to 64) and residents of the western United States tended to be in the heavy and very heavy user groups. Users in the light and moderate nutrient intake groups generally used only one broad-spectrum vitamin and mineral product. Users in the heavy and very heavy groups were typically taking two or more specialised vitamin and mineral products at a time as part of a personalised supplement regimen. Heavy and very heavy nutrient intakes were associated with more frequent visits to health-food stores, greater nutrition activity, and less physician involvement. Light and moderate nutrient intakes were more likely to be associated with a defensive interest in avoiding nutritional deficiencies.

QUESTIONS AND TASKS

1 What do you think the term 'vitamin and mineral supplements' means?

   Answer ....
   ....
   ....
   ....
   ....

2 What might be meant by nutritional deficiencies?

   Answer ....
   ....
   ....
   ....
   ....

CHAPTER 3 – Preparation for sport

NUTRITIONAL REQUIREMENTS

CASE STUDY 3.10
SPORTS DRINKS BOOST OLYMPIC ATHLETES

According to the 2004 West Europe Sports Drinks report from leading drinks consultancy Zenith International, issued to coincide with the opening of the 2004 Olympic Games, the sports drink market in western Europe sprinted past the €1000 million barrier in 2003, putting on a 27 per cent volume spurt to 477 million litres.

'More athletes are using sports drinks to improve their performance and the Olympics should help ensure double figure growth again in 2004,' commented Zenith research director Gary Roethenbaugh.

Germany is the leading national market, with a 26 per cent volume share, followed by Italy with 19 per cent and the UK with 15 per cent. The Netherlands has the highest consumption per person, with Olympic host Greece lagging well behind the overall average. PepsiCo's Gatorade is the brand champion, with 15 per cent of total volume. Coca-Cola's Powerade, however, is rapidly catching up, taking the silver medal in 2003 on 12 per cent, narrowly beating GlaxoSmithKline's Lucozade Sport in the final stretch.

Hypotonic sports drinks gained most momentum during 2002 and 2003, more than doubling their market share to 20 per cent. This reflects a trend towards less calorific, low-carbohydrate products, the growing appeal of sports drinks for female consumers and the rising number of people seeing sport as a means to losing weight. Nevertheless, isotonic drinks still led the field on 73 per cent, while hypertonic drinks accounted for the remaining 7 per cent.

Larger pack sizes are also contributing to market growth, with 50 cl PET bottles responsible for 62 per cent of volume sales, followed by 75 cl and 60 cl PET reaching a combined 19 per cent.

Concluding with detailed forecasts, Zenith foresees continuing strong growth, taking total western European consumption of sports drinks past 750 million litres by 2008. 'Greater product choice together with increasing consumer health awareness bode well for the future, but smaller brands risk being marginalised unless they focus on effectively communicating their benefits,' Gary Roethenbaugh concluded.

QUESTIONS AND TASKS

1 What do you understand by the following terms:

   - Hypotonic ....
     ....

   - Isotonic ....
     ....

   - Hypertonic? ....
     ....

2 Why would it be best for athletes to avoid ingesting caffeine?

   Answer ....
   ....
   ....

CHAPTER 3 – Preparation for sport

NUTRITIONAL REQUIREMENTS

CASE STUDY 3.11
UK TEACHER WINS CALIFORNIA TO NEW YORK MARATHON

Primary-school teacher Bob Brown ran 50 miles a day for two months in order to win the US ultra-marathon, one of the biggest crowns in endurance running. During the 3100 mile race, Brown used five pairs of trainers and lost 2 stone in weight.

According to Brown his mental attitude was as important as his physical fitness. He endured the dry heat of the desert and the energy-sapping humidity of the east coast of America. In 1997, at the World Decatriathlon Championships (one of the toughest races known to man) he swam 24 miles, cycled 1120 miles and ran 262 miles in eight days and six hours.

QUESTIONS AND TASKS

The decatriathlon is an extreme sport in terms of its demands on the athlete. Find out more about his type of event and answer the following questions:

1. What is Le Defi Mondial de l'Endurance and where is it held?

   Answer ....
   ....
   ....
   ....

2. What is the Ultratriathlon Levis and where is it held?

   Answer ....
   ....
   ....
   ....

3. Where are the Ultraman World Championships held and what are the demands on the athletes?

   Answer ....
   ....
   ....
   ....

CHAPTER 3 – Preparation for sport

NUTRITIONAL REQUIREMENTS

CASE STUDY 3.12
GOLF FITNESS

Getting fit can help your golf game, and playing golf can help you get or stay fit. Here are the ways in which fitness, health and safety can be achieved:

- Warm up properly. Start slowly with some stretching exercises. Take a few half-speed swings before attempting a full-speed swing.
- Protect your skin from the sun. Wear a strong sun block and a cap, or at least a visor, to keep the sun off your face.
- Drink plenty of fluids. Take advantage of every water station. If you buy a beverage on the course, make it a sports drink such as Gatorade.
- Do not drink too much alcohol. Many golfers play as an excuse to drink beer. But alcohol dehydrates and disorients, both of which are bad during a round – and especially after a round.
- Lift with your legs. This applies to lifting golf bags in particular – bending at the waist to pick up your bag is an easy way to strain your back.
- Be aware! Golf clubs and golf balls can do a lot of damage if one strikes you.
- Consult a professional golfer for help with golf-related ailments. Many pros can help with physical fitness or refer you to a specialist in golf-related injuries.
- If there is lightning anywhere in the area, get off the course immediately! People carrying golf clubs in their hands are at great risk from lightning.

QUESTIONS AND TASKS

1 Suggest some health and safety tips for golfers based on the information given in the case study.

   Answer ....
   ....
   ....
   ....
   ....
   ....
   ....

BTEC First Sport Tutor Support Pack © Jon Sutherland, Nelson Thornes Ltd, 2005

WORKSHEET 2 PSYCHOLOGICAL FACTORS: YOUTH SPORTS MOTIVATION QUESTIONNAIRE

The following is a list of reasons that young people have given in answer to the question, 'Why do you play sports?' Please look at each reason and decide whether you agree with it. If a reason is one for which you play your sport, you should place a mark in the box under 'I agree'. If it is not one of the reasons you play your sport, you should place a mark in the box under 'I do not agree'. If you are not sure if it is a reason you play your sport, you should place a mark in the box under 'I'm not sure'.

		I agree	I'm not sure	I do not agree
1	I can be active.	☐	☐	☐
2	I learn new skills.	☐	☐	☐
3	I can get better.	☐	☐	☐
4	It helps me be fit.	☐	☐	☐
5	It helps me be healthy.	☐	☐	☐
6	I make and have friends.	☐	☐	☐
7	It is exciting.	☐	☐	☐
8	My parents want me to play.	☐	☐	☐
9	I can win competitions.	☐	☐	☐
10	I'm good at it.	☐	☐	☐
11	It makes me feel special.	☐	☐	☐
12	It helps me with life.	☐	☐	☐
13	I have fun.	☐	☐	☐
14	I can be part of a team.	☐	☐	☐
15	It helps me look good.	☐	☐	☐
16	It gives me energy.	☐	☐	☐
17	I can compete against others.	☐	☐	☐
18	I learn about myself.	☐	☐	☐
19	It helps me get along with others.	☐	☐	☐
20	I learn self-control.	☐	☐	☐
21	It will help me be a good athlete.	☐	☐	☐
22	My friends want me to play.	☐	☐	☐
23	I will earn money for sports in the future.	☐	☐	☐
24	I will be chosen for a better team.	☐	☐	☐
25	It makes me feel good.	☐	☐	☐
26	It gives me confidence.	☐	☐	☐
27	I like this sport.	☐	☐	☐
28	I like my coach.	☐	☐	☐

WORKSHEET 2 (CONT.) PSYCHOLOGICAL FACTORS: YOUTH SPORTS MOTIVATION QUESTIONNAIRE

QUESTIONS AND TASKS

1. Look at the list and write down the three most important reasons that you play your sport.

   Answer ....
   ....
   ....
   ....

2. Copy at least 25 of these questionnaires and find people up to the age of 21 to complete them.

3. Look at your results and find out the most common reasons for taking part in sporting activities. What are the most common reasons?

   Answer ....
   ....
   ....
   ....
   ....
   ....
   ....

WORKSHEET 3 PSYCHOLOGICAL FACTORS: INVERTED U THEORY DIAGRAM

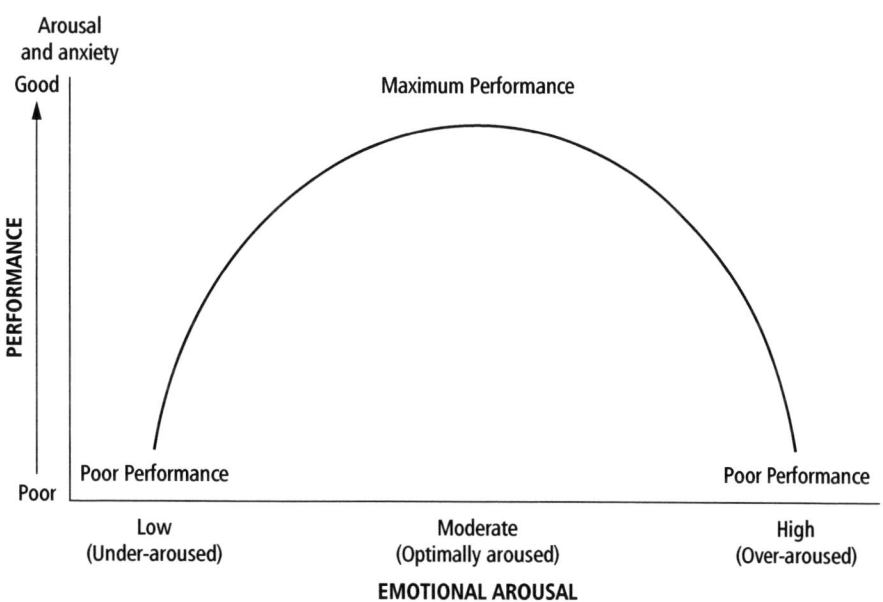

QUESTIONS AND TASKS

1   What is the inverted U theory and what does it tell you about athletes?

    Answer ....

    ....

    ....

    ....

CHAPTER 3 – Preparation for sport

WORKSHEET 4 PSYCHOLOGICAL FACTORS: QUESTIONNAIRE – PERSONALITY TESTS

What type of student or sports person are you? Rate yourself out of 10 for each of the following questions. If you agree with the statement give yourself a high score. If you disagree with the statement give yourself a low score.

Score

1 I do not believe you should express your feelings. ☐

2 I am never late. ☐

3 I am very competitive. ☐

4 I do not need hobbies; I have my course and sport. ☐

5 I walk, talk and eat quickly. ☐

6 I am always in a hurry. ☐

7 I have lots to do all at the same time. ☐

Total ☐

If you scored 55 or more then you cannot sit still without feeling guilty, you always try to fit the maximum number of things into a day. You run around doing 10 things at a time and find it very difficult to listen.

If you scored 40 or less then you usually stay cool and calm and you do not think you need to prove yourself.

CHAPTER 3 – Preparation for sport

PSYCHOLOGICAL FACTORS

CASE STUDY 3.13
MARAT SAFIN

It is one of Marat Safin's most endearing traits that you cannot trust him to do anything. From winning the US Open in 2002 and then stubbornly refusing to win anything else, to reaching the Australian Open final at the beginning of 2004 and then disappearing from view for much of the rest of the season, Safin confounds his critics and confuses his supporters.

Then, with no warning at all, he won two Masters Series titles in a fortnight. In Paris in November 2004 he won the BNP Paribas Masters for the third time in five years, beating Radek Stepanek 6–3, 7–6, 6–3, and adding the trophy to the Madrid Masters crown he acquired 14 days previously.

Since Safin began working with Peter Lundgren, Roger Federer's former coach, the Swede had been trying to get his charge to concentrate.

At the Tennis Masters Cup in November 2004, Safin kept the famed Russian temper under control and moved towards the trophy with an increased sense of purpose. Only once was there a hint that his attention would waver and he came through the crisis unscathed.

From a set and a break down, Stepanek, playing in his first final, tied on his bandana and started to attack. Safin responded by twiddling his racket, looking unhappy and dropping his serve. But Lundgren's new-improved Safin managed to screw down his concentration and get back to the business of winning by the time he had reached the tiebreak.

'Peter just tried to make me more focused,' Safin said. 'Just to be solid, try to do my stuff. Even though it doesn't go well, just keep going, and keep on trying. Most of it is mental toughness, just try to be there as long as you can.'

So Safin kept on going all the way to Houston and the Masters Cup.

QUESTIONS AND GUIDELINES

1 Mental concentration is extremely important in sport as can be seen in the case study. Why is concentration and toughness important to athletes?

   Answer ....

   ....

   ....

   ....

   ....

   ....

   ....

   ....

   ....

   ....

   ....

   ....

IVA REVISION AND PREPARATION

Students will need to do the following to meet the grading criteria of this unit:

- List the physical fitness and lifestyle factors of TWO contrasting athletes and comment on how these two areas affect their performance.
- Carry out fitness tests on an athlete and assess their level of fitness.
- Outline a two-week training programme for a sport.
- Prepare TWO dietary guidelines for two athletes to promote two of the following three athletic requirements: speed, endurance or power.
- List the psychological factors that affect BOTH training and performance.

ANSWERS AND GUIDELINES TO CASE STUDY 3.1

1   Aerobic literally means 'with oxygen'. During aerobic work the body is working at a level where the demands for oxygen and fuel can be met by the body's intake. The only waste products formed are carbon dioxide and water. These are removed as sweat and by breathing out.

   Aerobic endurance can subdivided as follows:
   - short aerobic – two minutes to eight minutes (lactic/aerobic)
   - medium aerobic – eight minutes to 30 minutes (mainly aerobic)
   - long aerobic – 30 minutes plus (aerobic).

   Aerobic endurance is developed through the use of continuous and interval running. Continuous duration runs improve maximum oxygen uptake and interval training improves the heart as a muscular pump.

2   Ideally a footballer's diet should take the following needs into account.

   A good diet for a footballer would include 55 per cent carbohydrate, 15 per cent protein and the rest fat and vitamins and minerals. Before exercise, a footballer should try to eat a balanced meal where two-thirds of what is on the plate is energy-giving carbohydrate (see table below).

   Drinking enough fluid is also extremely important for footballers. You have seen the physiotherapist with his water bottles and players refuelling whenever they can during a game. When you exercise you sweat, which is the body's way of cooling down. But in order to sweat, and so keep your body cool, you need plenty of water. That is why you should drink plenty before training or playing football even if you are not thirsty, and take a sip from a water bottle whenever possible. After exercise you should immediately refuel your body's water stocks. When you feel thirsty that is your body telling you to drink, but even if you do not feel parched you should drink at least two big glasses of water. Sports drinks are also good because as well as water they contain important sugars and salts which your body needs for exercise and also needs to replace after exercise. However, these are very expensive and you can make your own cheaper version by mixing half water, half orange juice and adding a pinch of salt.

ANSWERS AND GUIDELINES TO CASE STUDY 3.2

1   This group exercise should be used to reveal the relationships between the test results and other factors and that the results may well reveal disproportionate scores when compared with other factors such as age, gender and overall body mass.

CARBOHYDRATES	Energy for exercise comes from carbohydrates, and the best foods for carbohydrates are things like pasta, rice, bread and potatoes. Eating a meal which has plenty of at least one of these carbohydrates a few hours before playing a game or going out training will make a difference.
PROTEIN	Protein comes from lean, non-fatty meat, fish and poultry, as well as milk, cheese, yogurt and even some vegetables like beans. It is important for sportspeople because it helps the growth and repair of the body.
VITAMINS AND MINERALS	Found particularly in fresh fruit and vegetables, vitamins and minerals are very important for keeping the body healthy and fighting off germs. They are especially important if a sportsperson is doing a lot of exercise and pushing themselves to the limit. The aim should be to eat at least one piece of fruit a day, and fresh vegetables or salad with every meal.
FAT	Eating too much fatty food like chips, crisps and fast-food burgers is not good, either on or off the football pitch. Fat can cause people to be overweight and unhealthy, making them slower and less energetic on the pitch.

ANSWERS AND GUIDELINES TO CASE STUDY 3.3

1. BMI is not an accurate measure of healthy weight for everybody. If someone has a lot of muscle, they may have a BMI over 25 but very little body fat. Similarly, if someone has very little muscle, they may still have too much body fat even though they are in the correct weight range for their height.

   In either of these situations it can be helpful to look at body shape and composition.

   Where the fat is stored on the body relates to the risk to health. Carrying fat around the middle of the body, giving the body an apple shape, is a greater risk to health than carrying it around the bottom and thighs, which gives a pear shape. Measuring the waist gives a rough guide to whether it is necessary to lose some weight. The at-risk waist measurement is 102 cm (40 inches) for men and 88 cm (35 inches) for women. For people under 150 cm (4 feet 11 inches) tall, a smaller measurement will apply.

   Measuring how much of the body weight is made up of fat can be a useful way of monitoring weight. A local gym or leisure centre may be able to arrange a body composition test. The usual methods of measurement use skin fold callipers or an electronic monitor which passes a painless electric current through the body.

   Experts do not agree on what percentage of body fat is healthy and it varies depending on age and sex. The maximum should be 35 per cent fat for men and 40 per cent for women.

ANSWERS AND GUIDELINES TO CASE STUDY 3.4

1. Plyometrics are specialist exercises that enable a muscle to reach maximal strength in a short space of time. This works by stretching the muscle and then relying on its elastic properties to produce greater forces than are normally possible in the reflex contraction (as the muscle returns to its resting length). In order to achieve this greater muscular force, the muscle must contract within the shortest possible time following lengthening.

2. Ideally, the following should be taken into account before this form of training is used:
   - Ensure you warm up thoroughly.
   - If muscular or joint problems are experienced, stop immediately.
   - Wear quality footwear that provides ankle support and has adequate, but not too much, cushioning in the sole.
   - Use a flat landing surface that has good shock-absorbing properties. Surfaces such as sprung-loaded floors are not appropriate (they interfere with the elastic properties of the muscle as it operates in a plyometric), nor are heavily cushioned surfaces such as crash mats (they absorb too much energy and ruin the stretch-shortening mechanism of the exercise). The best surface is a grass field or tartan athletics track.
   - If boxes or benches are used, make sure they are sturdy and have a non-slip surface.
   - Make sure there is adequate space for training. Do not put yourself at risk from obstacles (or other people) that may encroach on the activity.
   - The work should be of high quality, therefore rest adequately between sets.
   - Technique is very important: if in doubt, seek appropriate coaching. As with sprinting, the aim is to land on the balls of the feet and use this area of the foot to apply force to the floor in order to accelerate the body off the ground. The contact pattern should therefore be ball-heel-ball.

ANSWERS AND GUIDELINES TO CASE STUDY 3.5

1.
   - Watson fartlek for 10 km, 5 km, 3 km and cross-country.
   - Saltin fartlek for 1500 m, 5 km and 3 km.
   - Astrand fartlek for 800 m.
   - Gerschler fartlek for getting fit quickly when combined with steady running.
   - Hill fartlek for cross-country.
   - Whistle fartlek for sessions over a grass area of 1200 m circumference.

   A fartlek session for games players should use running and also jogging and walking to fit in with the demands of the sport. After all, no soccer player actually runs for the whole 90 minutes of a match, the pace is varied. Similarly, the direction of work should not always be straight ahead. This may be important for the track runner who has to cover the ground as quickly as possible in one direction, but the games player has to go forwards, backwards and from side to side. This must all be taken into account if the training session is going to mimic accurately the pattern experienced in a match.

ANSWERS AND GUIDELINES TO CASE STUDY 3.6

1. Interval running enables the athlete to improve the workload by interspersing heavy bouts of fast running with recovery periods of slower jogging. The athlete runs hard over any distance up to 1 km and then has a period of easy jogging. During the run lactic acid is produced and a state of oxygen debt is reached. During the interval (recovery) the heart and lungs are still stimulated as they try to pay back the debt by supplying oxygen to help break down the lactates. The stresses put on the body cause an adaptation including capillarisation, strengthening of the heart muscles, improved oxygen uptake and improved buffers to lactates. All this leads to improved performance, in particular within the cardiovascular system.

2. Before undertaking interval training a few simple rules should be understood:
   - Undertake a period of continuous running before starting interval running.
   - Consider the various elements of the session and ensure they are within the scope of the athlete.
   - Consider the length of the work interval: longer gives a better effect.
   - The pace should be comfortable, raising the athlete's heart rate to the required per cent of maximum heart rate (MHR).
   - The number of repetitions should reflect the condition and age of the athlete.
   - The rest interval should enable the athlete to jog and bring the heart rate down to near 100–110 beats per minute.
   - Improvements can be made by altering any of the above variables, however the coach should only change one variable at a time.
   - All changes should be gradual in nature and take place over a period of time.
   - Ensure the surface to be run on is flat and even. It is usual to do interval training on a track although it can be done on good-quality grass playing fields. Roads are not a suitable surface because of the pounding effect.

ANSWERS AND GUIDELINES TO CASE STUDY 3.7

1. The FITT principle is most commonly used in the weight-loss industry, although it is also used as part of strength and weight-training recommendations. The standard recommendation is as follows:
   - Frequency – five to six times per week.
   - Intensity – moderate to high.
   - Time – anywhere from 15 to 40 minutes.
   - Type – just about any exercise.

2. Exercises like walking, jogging, swimming, cycling, stair climbing, aerobics and rowing are very effective to improve cardiovascular fitness.

3. To improve muscular strength the best exercises include the use of free weights, machine weights and body-weight exercises like push-ups, chin-ups and dips.

ANSWERS AND GUIDELINES TO WORKSHEET I FITNESS TESTS

This exercise should alert the student to their overall preparation and fitness for a sporting activity. It should provide useful information in order that the student can consider these factors in the future.

ANSWERS AND GUIDELINES TO CASE STUDY 3.8

1. During the process of digestion the proteins in our food are broken down into their constituent amino acids, which are in turn absorbed by the blood capillaries and transported to the liver. The amino acids are then synthesised into proteins or stored as fat or glycogen for energy. Each gram of protein produces approximately 4 kcal. Many proteins function as enzymes, and others:
   - form the structural framework of various parts of the body such as keratin in skin and hair
   - function as hormones such as insulin
   - serve as antibodies
   - transport vital substances throughout the body, e.g. haemoglobin transports oxygen
   - serve as contractile elements in muscle tissues, e.g. actin and myosin.

2. A person's digestive system converts the carbohydrates in food into glucose, a form of sugar carried in the blood and transported to cells for energy. The glucose, in turn, is broken down into carbon dioxide and water. Any glucose not used by the cells is converted into glycogen – another form of carbohydrate that is stored in the muscles and liver. However, the body's glycogen capacity is limited to about 350 grams. Once this maximum has been reached, any excess glucose is quickly converted into fat. Construct the main meal so that the bulk of it is carbohydrates and there are small amounts of protein such as meat, poultry and fish. The

extra protein and vitamins that an athlete needs are in the starchy carbohydrates.

ANSWERS AND GUIDELINES TO CASE STUDY 3.9

1. Vitamins serve crucial functions in almost all bodily processes (immune, hormonal and nervous systems) and must be obtained from food or supplements as our bodies are unable to make vitamins. There are 13 vitamins classified as either water-soluble (C and B complex) or fat-soluble (A, D, E and K).

   Approximately 4 per cent of the body's mass consists of minerals. They are classified as trace minerals (the body requires less than 100 mg/day) and major minerals (the body requires more than 100 mg/day). Minerals can be found in water and soil and therefore in root plants and animals. The trace minerals are iron, zinc, copper, selenium, iodine, fluorine and chromium. The major minerals are sodium, potassium, calcium, phosphorus, magnesium, sulphur and chlorine.

2. Vitamins are essential to the body and their absence causes deficiency diseases. The table below shows some common vitamins, their sources, causes for deficiency and symptoms.

ANSWERS AND GUIDANCE TO CASE STUDY 3.10

1. A hypotonic drink contains less carbohydrate (CHO) concentration than the blood, therefore it can be absorbed well by the body and is the type of drink used during exercise when rehydration is more important than providing fuel.

   Isotonic drinks contain a higher CHO solution that is similar to blood. Again the body

Vitamin	Value	Deficiency problems
Thiamine (Vitamin B1)	Found abundantly in all varieties of food and is rapidly destroyed with cooking.	Deficiency symptoms can be tingling and numbness of fingers and toes.
Riboflavin (Vitamin B2)	Found in milk, meat, fish, leafy vegetables and is also destroyed with cooking.	Deficiency causes sore mouth, apthous ulcers and anaemia.
Niacin (Vitamin B5)	Found in wholegrain cereals, nuts, fish, meat.	Deficiency can be associated with a high intake of maize. Symptoms are rapid loss of weight, diarrhoea, fatigue and sometimes even severe loss of memory (dementia).
Pyridoxin (Vitamin B6)	Found in meat, vegetables and wholegrain cereals.	Symptoms of deficiency are seborrhoeic dermatitis (a dandruff-like condition of scalp, eyebrows), cuts on the lips (chelitis), burning sensation of the tongue, tingling and numbness of hands and legs.
Cobalamine (Vitamin B12)	Found in kidney, eggs and milk. Cobalamine is an essential intrinsic factor required for the formation of haemoglobin.	Deficiency can be found in patients with impaired gastric absorption and pancreatic diseases. Symptoms are anaemia, low blood pressure, tingling and numbness of extremities, redness and burning of tongue (glossitis).
Ascorbic acid (Vitamin C)	Found in fresh vegetables and citrus fruits.	Deficiency can cause bleeding gums, delayed healing of colds, purpura (bleeding disorder).
Folic acid	Found in green, leafy vegetables.	Deficiency symptoms include megaloblastic anaemia, glossitis, chelitis.
Vitamin A	Found in animal products (offal, dairy produce etc.), dark green and orange vegetables etc.	Deficiency causes dryness of eyes and skin, night blindness, corneal ulcers.
Vitamin D	Found in milk, fish, eggs and butter.	Inadequate exposure to sunlight also can cause deficiency. In children it causes rickets and in adults osteomalacia (softening of bones), muscle weakness and muscular cramps.

absorbs these drinks quite well but their main advantage is the higher glucose solution, which provides some CHO to help with refuelling during endurance exercise.

A hypertonic drink contains a high CHO and electrolyte (sodium etc.) solution and absorption of fluid will be slow in relation to water. These drinks are best used after exercise to replenish lost CHO and energy stores.

2. Caffeinated beverages should be kept to a minimum because of the diuretic effect. This is why cola is not a good form of hydration. Neat orange juice should not be used as a form of hydration as its CHO concentration is too high. For an effective isotonic drink it should be diluted with water in a ratio of 1:1 with an added pinch of salt to help absorption.

ANSWERS AND GUIDELINES TO CASE STUDY 3.11

1. The World Endurance Challenge is a triple iron man distance event held in Le Fontanil (near Grenoble), France.

2. This is a double iron man distance race in Levis, Quebec, Canada. It was held for the first time on 21 July 2000 and entailed a 7.6 km swim in the St Lawrence River, a 360 km cycle on a city street circuit closed to traffic (164 laps of 2.16 km), and a 84.4 km run on closed streets (38 laps of 2.2 km).

3. It is held in Hawaii. It is a three-day stage triathlon circumnavigating the Big Island of Hawaii. Day one is a 10 km (6.2 miles) ocean swim from Konas's Kailua Pier to Keauhou Bay, followed by a 90 mile cycle (with 4000 feet climb at Volcanoes National Park). Day two is a 171.4 mile cycle from Volcanoes National Park to Hawi. The last day is a double marathon run (52.4 miles) along the Ironman Hawaii bike course.

ANSWERS AND GUIDELINES TO CASE STUDY 3.12

1. A number of different suggestions could be made including the following:
   - Try a wide-brimmed straw hat rather than a golf cap or visor. The full brim will help protect the neck as well as the face from the sun.
   - Use a double-strap golf bag instead of a single strap when walking. The double-strap bag distributes the weight more evenly across your back and shoulders.
   - Wear comfortable, well-fitting golf shoes. Ill-fitting shoes can cause pain and long-term problems.

ANSWERS AND GUIDELINES TO WORKSHEET 2 YOUTH SPORTS MOTIVATION QUESTIONNAIRE

This activity requires some organisation and planning. The results should provide students with useful background information regarding motivation and will be of value for the IVA.

ANSWERS AND GUIDELINES TO WORKSHEET 3 INVERTED U THEORY

1. An alternative approach to drive theory is known as the inverted U theory. It predicts a relationship between arousal and performance and approximates to an inverted U shape. The theory is that as arousal is increased then performance improves, but only up to a certain point (top of the inverted U). If the athlete's arousal is increased beyond that point then performance diminishes.

ANSWERS AND GUIDELINES TO WORKSHEET 4 QUESTIONNAIRE: PERSONALITY TESTS

This simple set of questions has a fun element to it, but it does indicate to students their personal drives and approaches to the course and sport.

ANSWERS AND GUIDELINES TO CASE STUDY 3.13

1. This case study and questions infer what is known as mental imagery. In effect this means:
   - To see success. Many athletes 'see' themselves achieving their goals on a regular basis, both performing skills at a high level and seeing the desired performance outcomes.
   - To motivate. Before or during training sessions, calling up images of goals for that session, or of a past or future competition or competitor, can serve a motivational purpose. These can provide vivid reminders of objectives, which can result in increased intensity in training.
   - To perfect skills. It is often used to facilitate the learning and refinement of skills or skill

sequences. The best athletes 'see' and 'feel' themselves performing perfect skills, programs, routines, or plays on a regular basis.

- To familiarise. It can be effectively used to familiarise yourself with all kinds of things, such as a competition site, a race course, a complex play pattern or routine, a pre-competition plan, an event focus plan, a media interview plan, a refocusing plan, or the strategy you plan to follow.
- To set the stage for performance. Using mental imagery is often an integral part of the pre-competition plan which helps set the mental stage for a good performance. Athletes do a complete mental run through of the key elements of their performance. This helps draw out their desired pre-competition feelings and focus. It also helps to keep negative thoughts from interfering with a positive pre-game focus.
- To refocus. It can help to refocus when the need arises. For example, if a warm-up is feeling sluggish, imagery of a previous best performance or previous best event can help get things back on track. Imagery can also be used as a means of refocusing within the event, by imagining what you should focus on and feeling that focus.

CHAPTER 4: The body in sport

The information on this page is intended to help you plan and deliver your lessons using BTEC First Sport *by John Honeybourne.*

OVERVIEW

This chapter looks at how the body responds before, during and after exercise. Students will look at both the skeletal and muscular system and how they combine to produce movement during sports activities. Students will also look at the cardiovascular and respiratory systems.

This does require the students to grasp some basic scientific concepts, although they are focused towards sports activities and events. The primary goals of the unit are:

- To explain the structure of the skeletal system and its role in sports movement.
- To identify the major muscle groups and their role in sports movement.
- To identify the structure and function of the cardiovascular and respiratory systems.
- To investigate the short-term effect of exercise on those systems.

ADVICE AND GUIDANCE TO STUDENTS

This chapter looks at the science behind sports movement, including the skeletal system, the major muscle groups and the cardiovascular and respiratory systems. The unit also looks at the effects of exercise on both the cardiovascular and respiratory systems. In order to appreciate what is required in this unit's IVA, the following table outlines the key grading areas:

PASS	To obtain a MERIT do this as well	To obtain a DISTINCTION do this as well
Describe the structure and function of the skeletal, cardiovascular and respiratory systems.	Compare muscles and joint functions and their effect on movement.	Critically analyse these joints and muscles and their long-term effects on movement.
For three contrasting sports activities produce and use a checklist of muscles, joints and movement patterns.	Not applicable.	Not applicable.
Using teacher support, identify and use two tests to demonstrate breathing and changes in oxygen and carbon dioxide levels.	Explain and use the tests.	Analyse the relationship between activity and changes in these levels.
Identify immediate responses of the body to different sports exercise.	Explain and compare responses.	Critically analyse the responses and draw conclusions.

CHAPTER 4 – The body in sport

SUGGESTED LESSON PLAN

TOPIC	HOURS	ACTIVITY TO USE	PAGE
Skeletal system	7	Worksheet 5 The skull	91
The skeleton		Worksheet 6 The skeleton	92
The spine		Worksheet 7 The spine	93
The hand		Worksheet 8 The hand	94
The knee joint	7	Worksheet 9 The knee joint	95
Cartilage	2	Worksheet 10 Cartilage	96
Types of movement	3	Worksheet 11 Types of movement	97
Major muscles Muscles of the body	2	Worksheet 12 Muscles of the body (anterior view)	98
		Worksheet 13 Muscles of the body (posterior view)	99
The eye		Worksheet 14 Muscles of the eye	100
Functions of muscles	7	Worksheet 15 Functions of muscles	101
		Worksheet 16 Levers and energy needs for contraction	102
Cardiovascular and respiratory systems			
Structure of the heart	2	Worksheet 17 Structure of the heart	103
Function of the heart	2	Worksheet 18 Function of the heart	104
Arteries and veins	3	Worksheet 19 Arteries	105
		Worksheet 20 Veins	106
Respiratory system	3	Worksheet 21 Respiratory system	107
The mechanics of breathing	2	Worksheet 22 Mechanics of breathing	108
Short-term effects of exercise Effects of exercise	4	Worksheet 23 Effects of exercise	109
		Case Study 4.1 Lifestyle modification	110
Muscular systems and exercise	2	Worksheet 24 Muscular systems and exercise	111
Tests	2	Case Study 4.2 Air is essential to life	112
IVA revision and preparation	7		114

ANSWERS TO PROGRESS CHECK (PAGE 115, BTEC FIRST SPORT)

1   Name the four main functions of the human skeleton.

Answer
The four main functions of the human skeleton are:

- to provide support and shape to the body
- to allow movement of the body by providing sites for muscle attachment
- to protect the internal organs
- to produce red and white blood cells.

2   Describe the synovial joint. Choose one such joint and explain how it functions in a sports activity.

Answer
A knee joint is an example of a synovial joint. The synovial fluid provides lubrication. It allows a wide range of movement and is the most common type of joint.

3   Describe cartilage and what its function is in the human body.

Answer
Cartilage is soft, connective tissue consisting of three different types:

- yellow elastic cartilage, which is flexible (e.g. the earlobe)
- hyaline/blue articular cartilage, which protects the surface of bones and allows movement between bones
- white fibrocartilage, which is tough tissue that effectively acts as a shock absorber.

89

4 Give an example of a sports movement that involves flexion.

Answer
When a tennis player hits a forehand shot, the arm shows flexion at the elbow. It is essentially a decrease in the angle around a joint.

5 Name three major muscles and describe their functions.

Answer
Students could choose from triceps, biceps, deltoids, pectorals, trapezius, gluteals, hamstrings, gastrocnemius, latissimus dorsi or abdominals. The latter two are the broad back muscle and the muscles around the trunk, which help to turn the upper body.

6 Give an example of a pair of muscles that work together. Say which is the agonist and which the antagonist.

Answer
The biceps and triceps at the arm joint. The biceps bend the arm by contracting and the triceps relax. When the arm straightens the opposite occurs.

7 Name and describe the three main levers.

Answer
There are three different classes of levers, which are:

- first class – such as the neck joint
- second class – such as the plantar in the ankle
- third class – the most common form of lever, when the effort is between the fulcrum and the resistance.

8 Draw and label the main structures of the human heart.

Answer
1. Superior vena cava
2. Right atrium
3. Tricuspid valve
4. Right ventricle
5. Interventricular septum
6. Aorta
7. Pulmonary artery
8. Left atrium
9. Bicuspid valve
10. Left ventricle.

9 Describe what happens to air as a person breathes in while performing a sports activity.

Answer
The respiratory muscles contract, including the external intercostal muscles and the diaphragm. The external intercostal muscles are attached to the ribs and when they contract the ribs move upwards and outwards. The diaphragm contracts downwards and the thoracic cavity area increases. The lungs are pulled outwards by surface tension, and the pressure within the lungs decreases to less than the pressure outside the body. Gases move from areas of high pressure to low pressure so air is pulled into the lungs.

10 Give three short-term effects of exercise on the body.

Answer
Short-term effects of exercise include:

- a rise in the heart rate
- a rise in the rate of breathing.

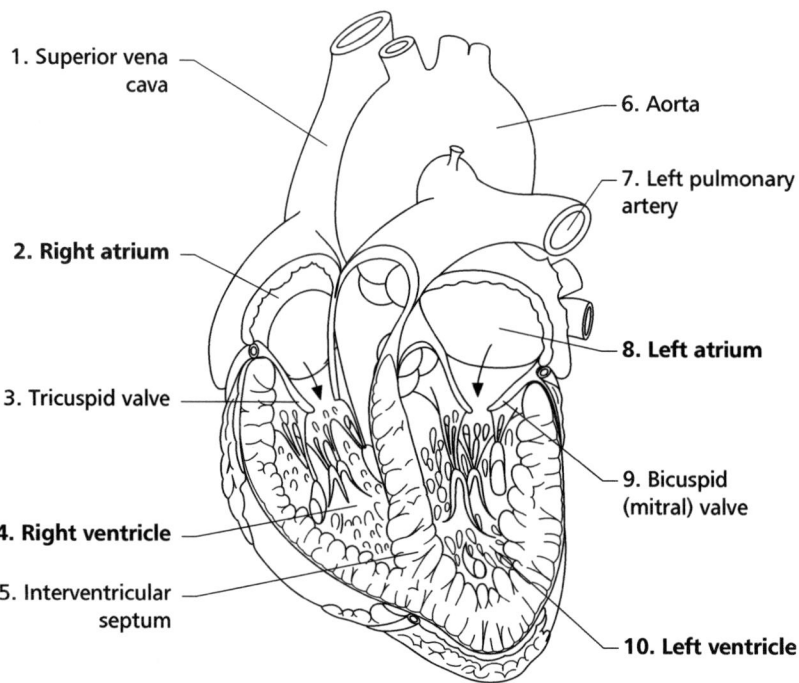

CHAPTER 4 – The body in sport

WORKSHEET 5 SKELETAL SYSTEM: THE SKULL

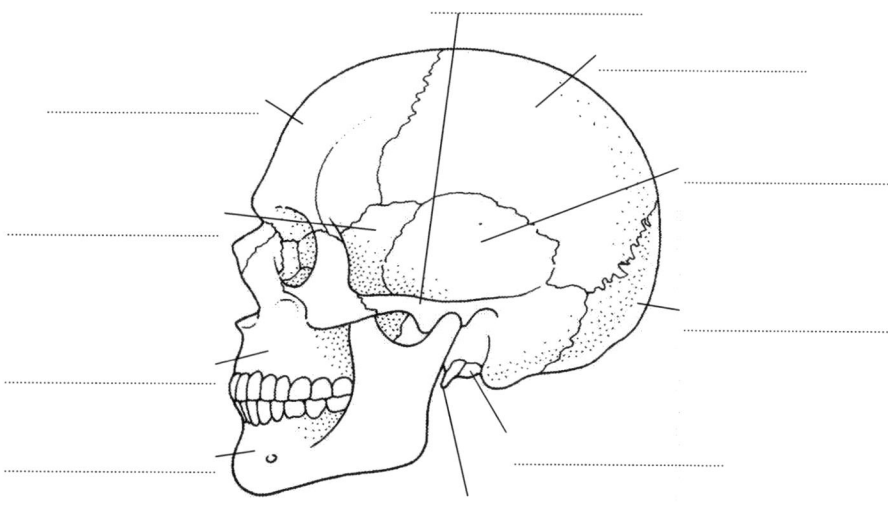

QUESTIONS AND TASKS

1 Look at the diagram of the skull and label the parts.

CHAPTER 4 – The body in sport

WORKSHEET 6 SKELETAL SYSTEM: THE SKELETON

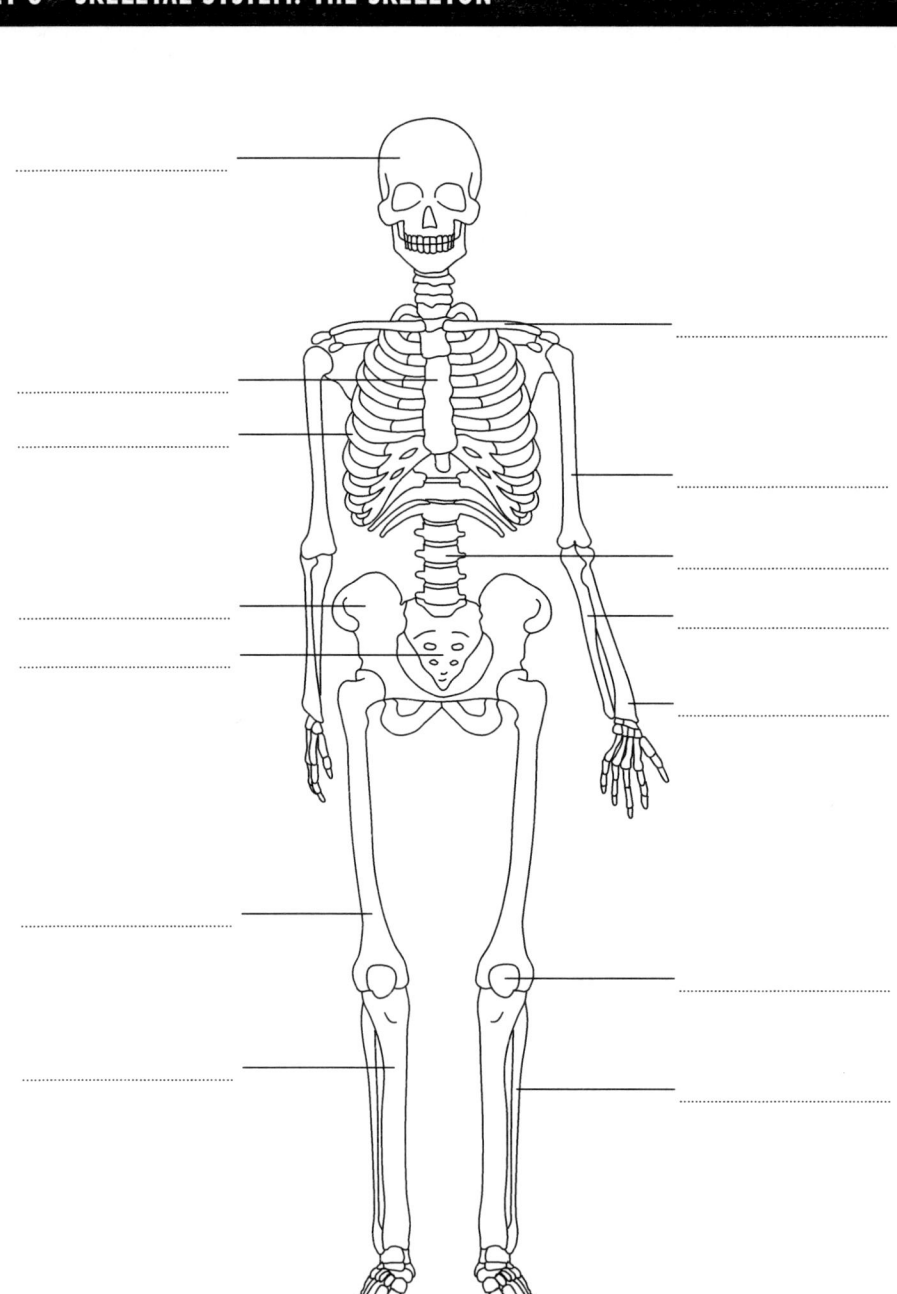

QUESTIONS AND TASKS

1. Look at the diagram of the skeleton and label the parts as indicated.

CHAPTER 4 – The body in sport

WORKSHEET 7 SKELETAL SYSTEM: THE SPINE

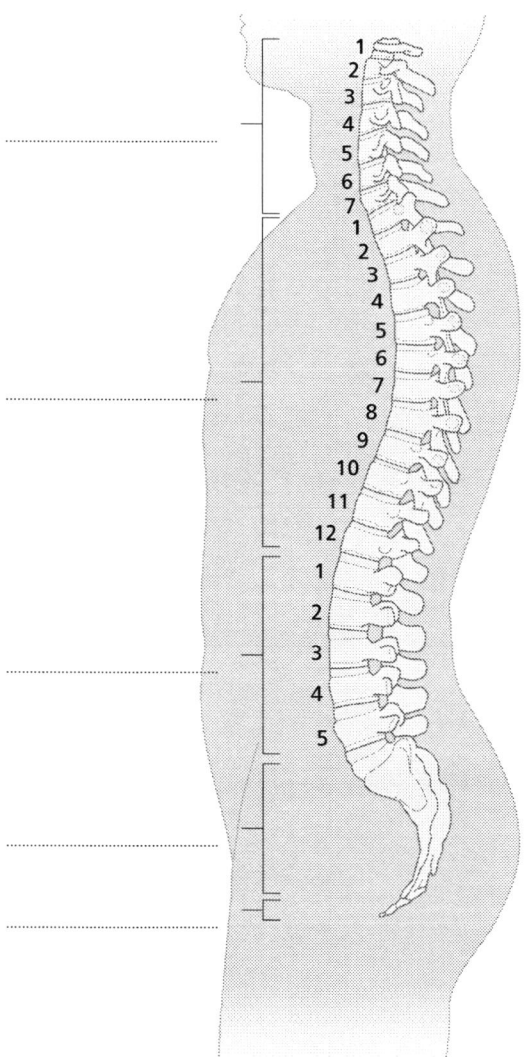

QUESTIONS AND TASKS

1   Look at the diagram of the spine and label it where indicated.

BTEC First Sport Tutor Support Pack © Jon Sutherland, Nelson Thornes Ltd, 2005

CHAPTER 4 – The body in sport

WORKSHEET 8 SKELETAL SYSTEM: THE HAND

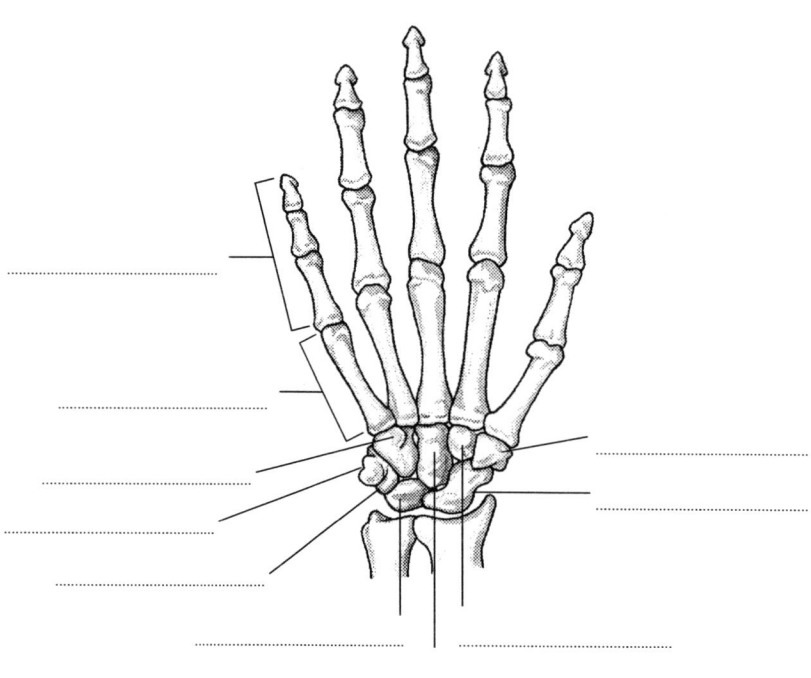

QUESTIONS AND TASKS

1   Label the parts of the hand where indicated.

CHAPTER 4 – The body in sport

WORKSHEET 9   SKELETAL SYSTEM: THE KNEE JOINT

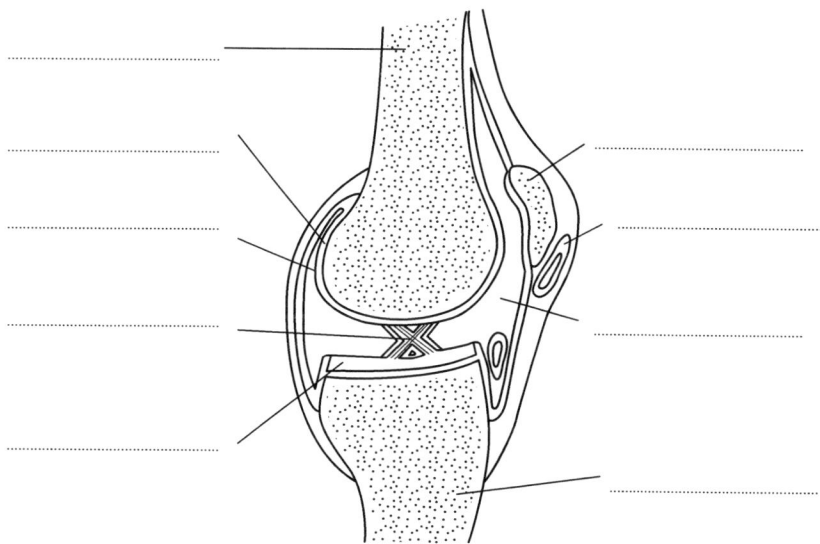

QUESTIONS AND TASKS

1   Name the parts of the knee joint where indicated.

CHAPTER 4 – The body in sport

WORKSHEET 10 SKELETAL SYSTEM: CARTILAGE

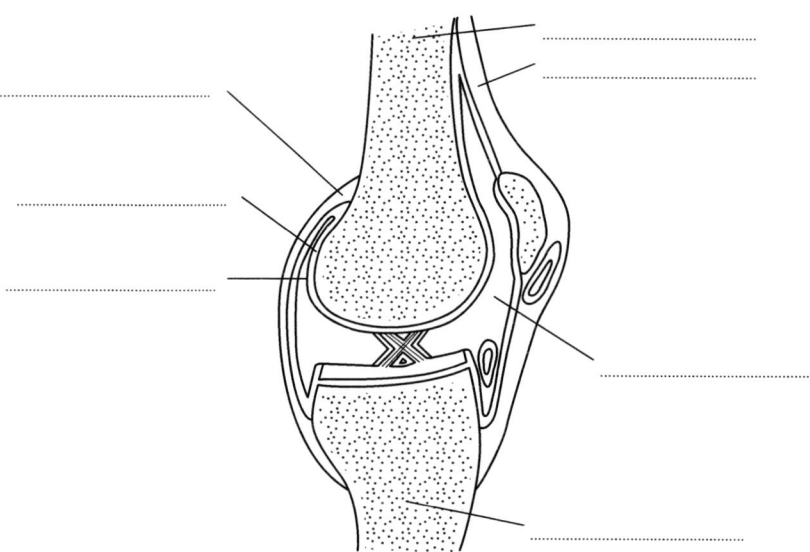

QUESTIONS AND TASKS

1 Look at the diagram of a normal joint and label where indicated.

CHAPTER 4 – The body in sport

WORKSHEET 11   SKELETAL SYSTEM: TYPES OF MOVEMENT

QUESTIONS AND TASKS

1 Look at the figure above and comment on the types of movement of the footballer in the picture.

   Answer ....

   ....

   ....

   ....

CHAPTER 4 – The body in sport

WORKSHEET 12 MAJOR MUSCLES: MUSCLES OF THE BODY (ANTERIOR VIEW)

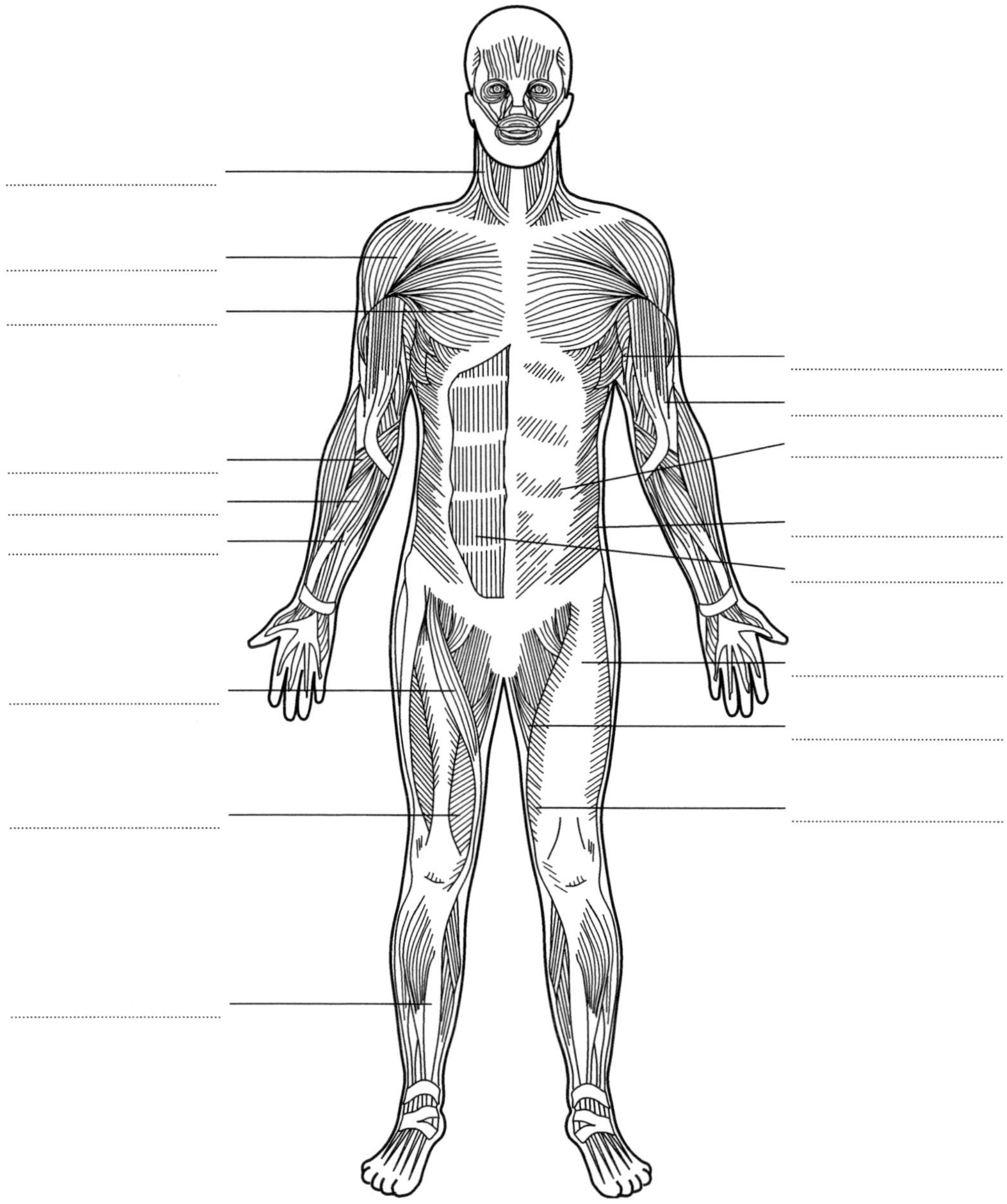

QUESTIONS AND TASKS

1 Look at the diagram and try to label as many of the muscles as possible.

CHAPTER 4 – The body in sport

WORKSHEET 13   MAJOR MUSCLES: MUSCLES OF THE BODY (POSTERIOR VIEW)

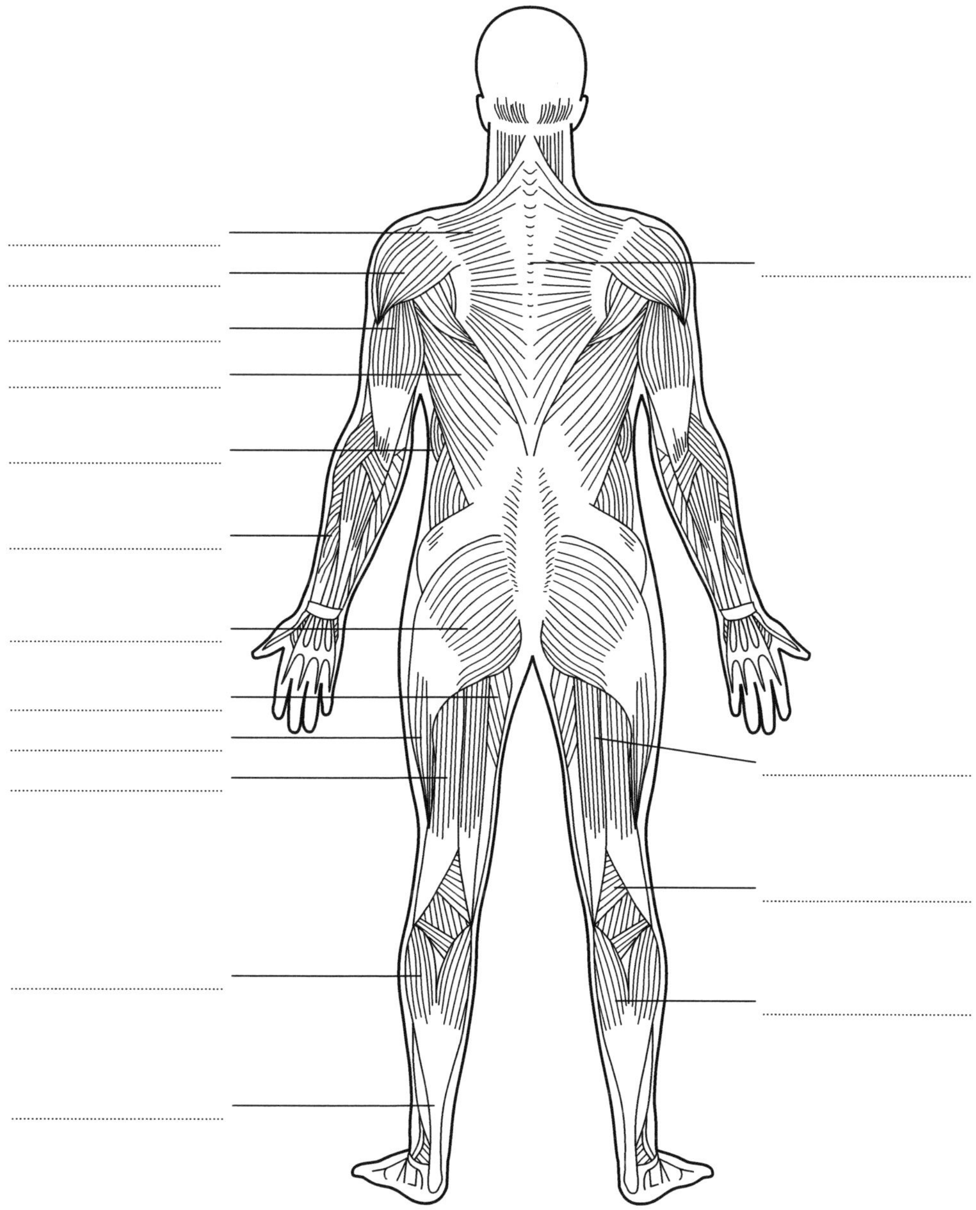

QUESTIONS AND TASKS

1   Look at the diagram and try to label as many of the muscles as possible.

BTEC First Sport Tutor Support Pack © Jon Sutherland, Nelson Thornes Ltd, 2005

WORKSHEET 14 MAJOR MUSCLES: MUSCLES OF THE EYE

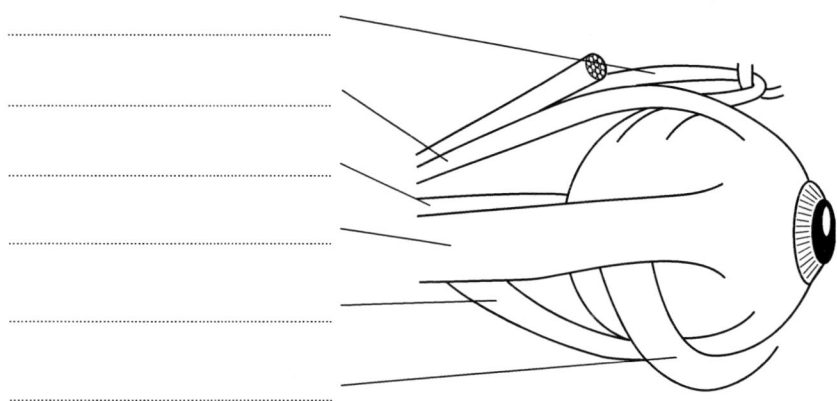

QUESTIONS AND TASKS

1. Look at the diagram of the eye and label as many of the parts as possible.

CHAPTER 4 – The body in sport

WORKSHEET 15 MAJOR MUSCLES: FUNCTIONS OF MUSCLES

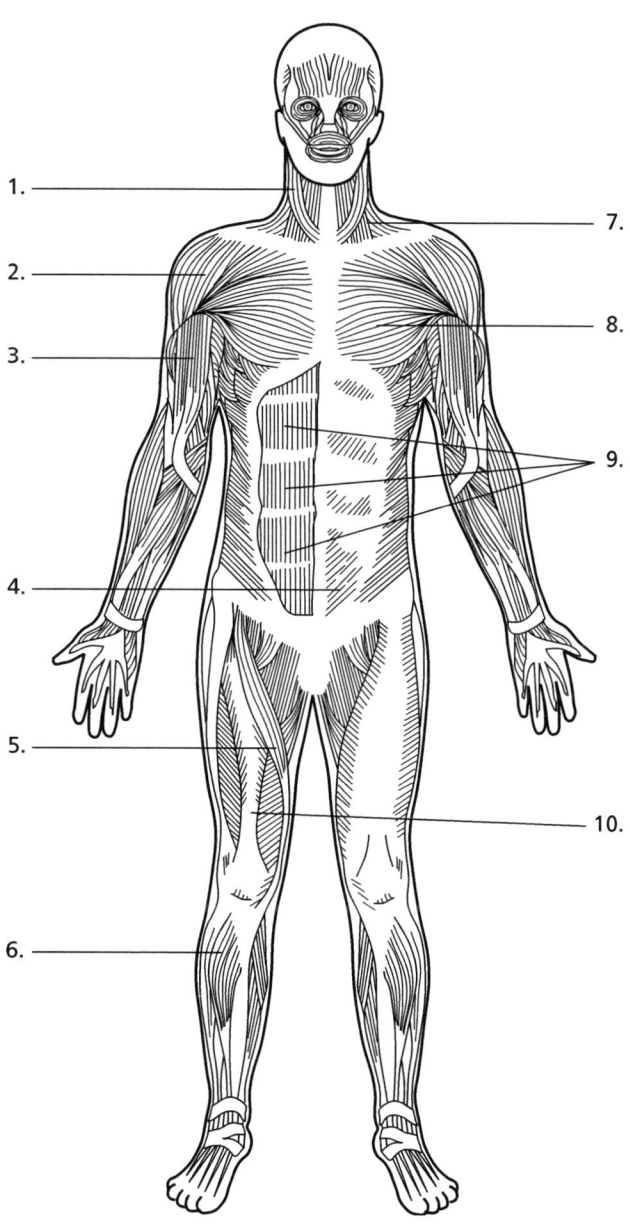

QUESTIONS AND TASKS

1   What are the muscle groups identified on the diagram?

   1 ....   6 ....
   2 ....   7 ....
   3 ....   8 ....
   4 ....   9 ....
   5 ....   10 ....

WORKSHEET 16 FUNCTIONS OF MUSCLES: LEVERS AND ENERGY NEEDS FOR CONTRACTION

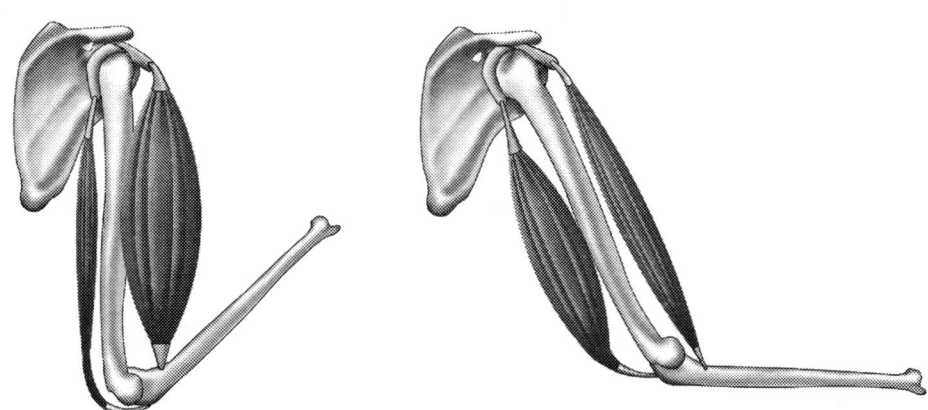

QUESTIONS AND TASKS

1. Look at the two diagrams of the arm. Label the diagrams and identify which of the muscles are relaxed and which are contracted in both cases.

WORKSHEET 17 CARDIOVASCULAR AND RESPIRATORY SYSTEMS: STRUCTURE OF THE HEART

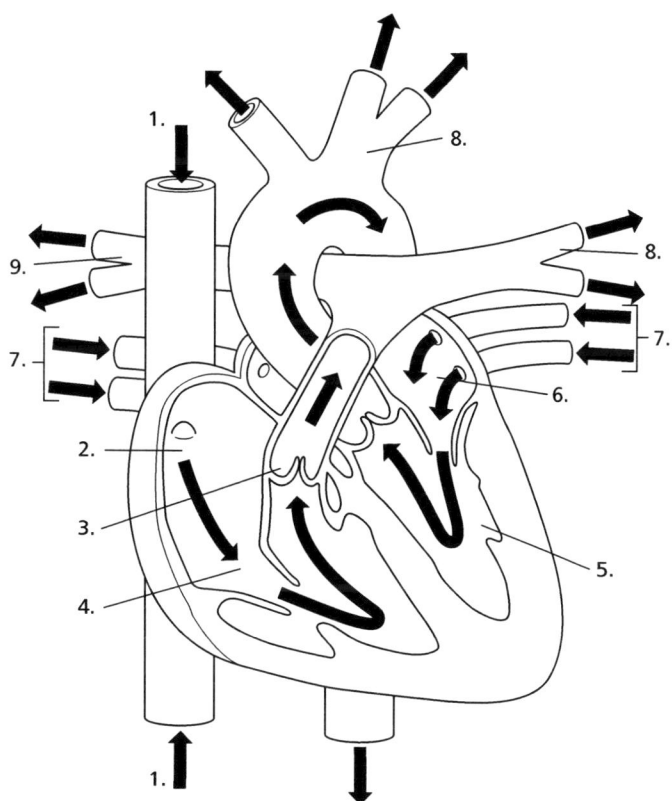

QUESTIONS AND TASKS

1. Look at the diagram and then complete the sentences using the words below:

   left ventricle valves
   right ventricle to the body
   from the lungs from the body
   left atrium right atrium
   to the lungs

   The 'double' pump of the human heart

1. Deoxygenated blood .... entering the heart.

2. The ....

3. The .... prevent blood flowing the wrong way when the atria and ventricles contract.

4. The ....

5. The thicker-walled ....

6. The ....

7. Oxygenated blood .... entering the heart.

8. Oxygenated blood leaving the heart and flowing ....

9. Deoxygenated blood leaving the heart and flowing ....

WORKSHEET 18 CARDIOVASCULAR AND RESPIRATORY SYSTEMS: FUNCTION OF THE HEART

QUESTIONS AND TASKS

1. Starting with the superior vena cava, place the following items in order according to the route taken by blood as it flows through the heart.
   - aorta
   - bicuspid valve
   - left atrium
   - left ventricle
   - lungs
   - pulmonary artery
   - pulmonary vein
   - right atrium
   - right ventricle
   - tricuspid valve.

   1 ....
   2 ....
   3 ....
   4 ....
   5 ....
   6 ....
   7 ....
   8 ....
   9 ....
   10 ....

CHAPTER 4 – The body in sport

WORKSHEET 19 CARDIOVASCULAR AND RESPIRATORY SYSTEMS: ARTERIES

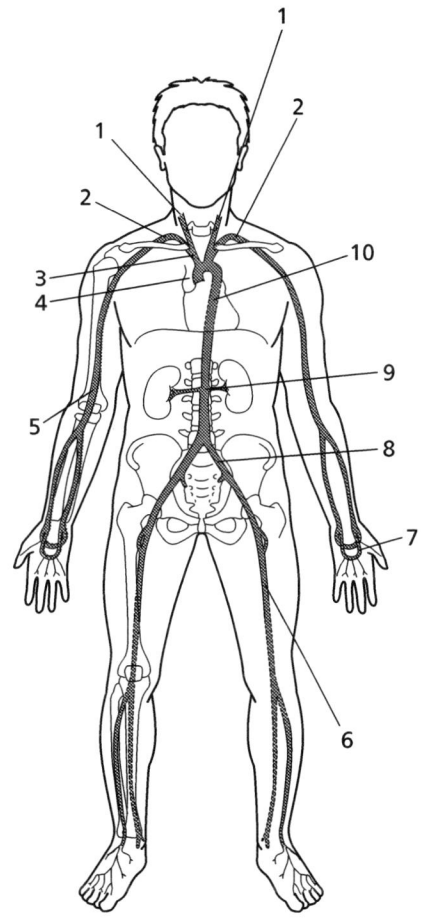

QUESTIONS AND TASKS

1 Look at the diagram and label as many of the arteries as possible.

1 ....

2 ....

3 ....

4 ....

5 ....

6 ....

7 ....

8 ....

9 ....

10 ....

BTEC First Sport Tutor Support Pack © Jon Sutherland, Nelson Thornes Ltd, 2005

WORKSHEET 20 CARDIOVASCULAR AND RESPIRATORY SYSTEMS: VEINS

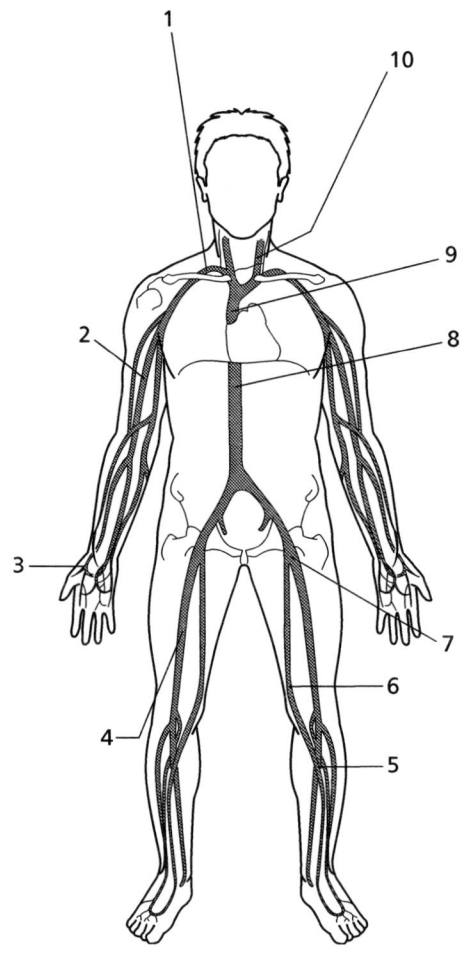

QUESTIONS AND TASKS

1 Look at the diagram and label as many of the veins as possible.

   1 ....
   2 ....
   3 ....
   4 ....
   5 ....
   6 ....
   7 ....
   8 ....
   9 ....
   10 ....

CHAPTER 4 – The body in sport

WORKSHEET 21 CARDIOVASCULAR AND RESPIRATORY SYSTEMS: RESPIRATORY SYSTEM

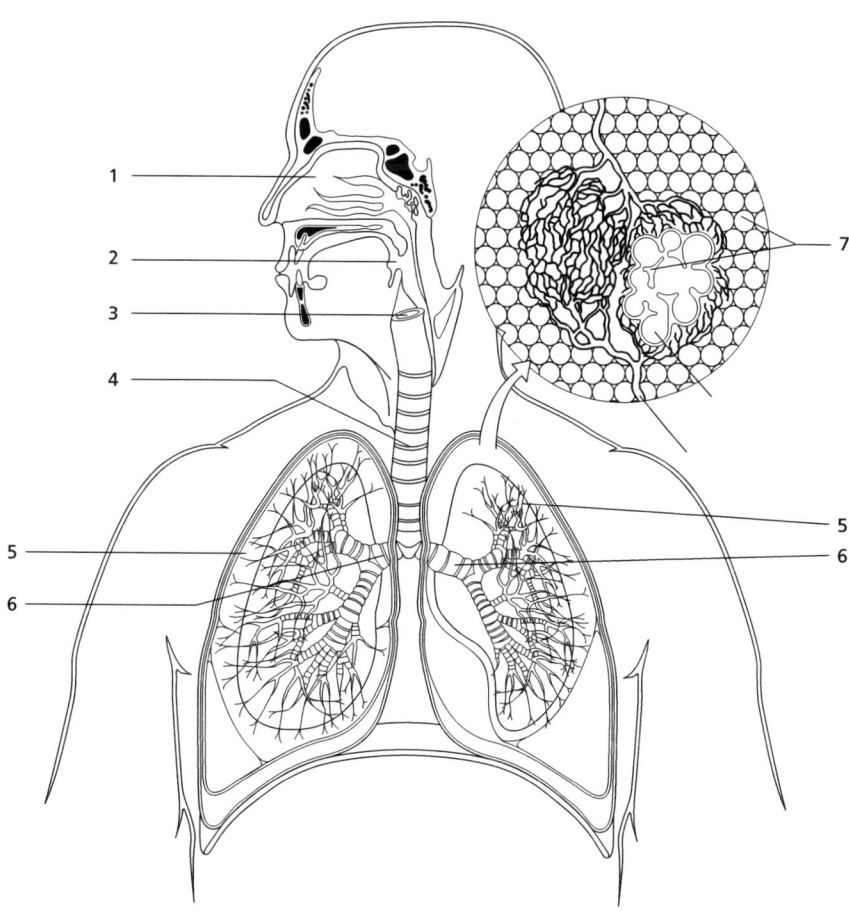

QUESTIONS AND TASKS

1 Look at the diagram of the respiratory system and label as many of the parts as possible.

   1 ....
   2 ....
   3 ....
   4 ....
   5 ....
   6 ....
   7 ....

CHAPTER 4 – The body in sport

WORKSHEET 22 CARDIOVASCULAR AND RESPIRATORY SYSTEMS: MECHANICS OF BREATHING

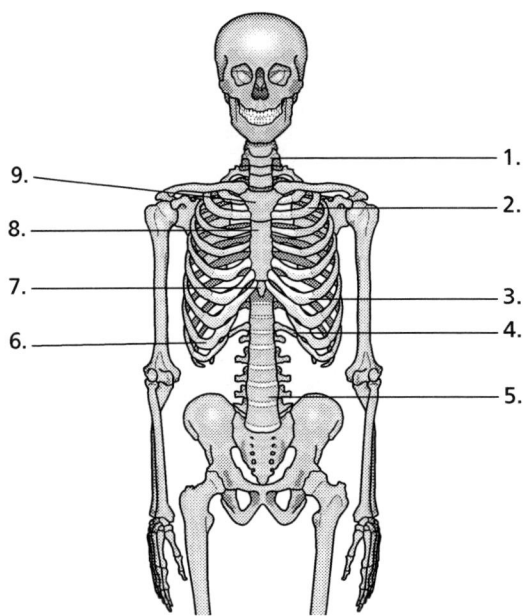

QUESTIONS AND TASKS

1 Look at the diagram of bones related to the mechanics of breathing and label as many as possible.

1 ....

2 ....

3 ....

4 ....

5 ....

6 ....

7 ....

8 ....

9 ....

BTEC First Sport Tutor Support Pack © Jon Sutherland, Nelson Thornes Ltd, 2005

CHAPTER 4 – The body in sport

WORKSHEET 23 SHORT-TERM EFFECTS OF EXERCISE: EFFECTS OF EXERCISE

QUESTIONS AND TASKS

1   Supplemental oxygen (from oxygen tanks) has been used by hikers climbing the Himalayas as well as by American football players after scoring touchdowns. Football players have generally stopped using supplemental oxygen because it is of little use, but it is useful to the mountain hiker. Explain why the oxygen is useful for hikers but not for footballers.

    Answer ....
    ....
    ....
    ....
    ....
    ....
    ....
    ....
    ....
    ....
    ....

CHAPTER 4 – The body in sport

SHORT-TERM EFFECTS OF EXERCISE

CASE STUDY 4.1
LIFESTYLE MODIFICATION

The importance of making lifestyle changes is frequently overlooked in managing hypertension, even though success in this area can be an important adjunct to lowering blood pressure and/or minimising the amount of medication required to control blood pressure. Lifestyle changes can also help prevent the development of hypertension in high-risk patients, such as patients who are overweight or obese.

The most scientifically established primary lifestyle changes are:

- weight loss
- reduced dietary sodium intake
- reduced alcohol intake
- increased physical activity.

Many studies show that a weight loss of only 10 to 15 pounds can result in a 5–10 mm Hg reduction in blood pressure. A reduction in sodium intake to below 100 mmol/day (2.3 g sodium) is necessary to lower blood pressure levels, and increased physical activity can lower blood pressure by improving fitness and enhancing weight loss. A 30–45-minute brisk walk done on most days can lower blood pressure significantly.

QUESTIONS AND TASKS

1. Why is lowering blood pressure so important in some cases?

   Answer ....

2. Suggest lifestyle changes to help reduce blood pressure.

   Answer ....

3. What do you understand by the term 'hypertension'?

   Answer ....

WORKSHEET 24   SHORT-TERM EFFECTS OF EXERCISE: MUSCULAR SYSTEMS AND EXERCISE

QUESTIONS AND TASKS

1. What are the long- and short-term effects of exercise on both the skeletal system and muscular system?

   Answer ....
   ....
   ....
   ....
   ....
   ....
   ....
   ....
   ....

SHORT-TERM EFFECTS OF EXERCISE

CASE STUDY 4.2
AIR IS ESSENTIAL TO LIFE

Humans and other animals use the oxygen they breathe along with the food they eat to produce energy. Increased physical activity raises the body's energy demand, increasing consumption of oxygen and nutrients. When we exert ourselves we notice an increase in breath rate. This is our respiratory system's response to increased energy demand.

More air flowing in and out of our lungs increases our exposure to air pollution. As a result, active children, adults, and athletes are more vulnerable to the unhealthy impacts of air pollution. During episodes of unhealthy levels of air pollution, public health officials advise reducing vigorous outdoor activities (for example soccer, running).

QUESTIONS AND TASKS

In order to carry out this task you will need the following:

- stopwatch, watch, clock, or timer
- worksheet to record and chart data.

Instructions:

1. Students should form research teams of 2–3 people. In the two-person groups, one student will time and record data while the other student will be the research subject. In the three-person groups, one student will time, one will record data, and the last will be the research subject. Each team member should take a turn as the research subject. The teacher or a student can be the timer for the whole class if there are not enough watches for each group.

2. Hand out a stopwatch and worksheet to each team. Each team should write their prediction on the worksheet, answering the question, 'Does a person breathe more or less during exercise?'

3. *Breathing at rest*: the subject is sitting down. The timer/recorder should give the subject the following instructions: 'When I say start, begin counting your breaths. Breathe normally.' The timer tells the subject to start. After one minute, the timer asks the subject how many breaths he or she has taken. The timer records the number on the worksheet under the subject's name.

4. *Breathing during exercise*: The timer/recorder should tell the subject, 'When I say start, begin jumping up and down. After 15 seconds, I will say stop. Stop jumping and immediately start counting your breaths.' The timer tells the subject to start. After 15 seconds, the timer tells the subject to stop jumping. After an additional 15 seconds, the timer asks the subject for a breath count. The recorder writes the number of breaths on the worksheet and multiplies it by four. The timer asks the subject, 'Were your breaths deeper while your exercised?' The recorder writes down the answer.

5. Repeat steps 3 and 4 until each team member has been the subject.

6. Comparing results. Ask each team to make a chart or graph showing the results of their research. One member of the team should present their prediction and results to the class. Discuss the variety of results. What other variables could cause widely varying results (physical condition, respiratory illness such as asthma)?

How could the results for the whole class could be shown?

CASE STUDY 4.2 (continued)

Does a person breathe more or less during exercise such as jumping up and down?

How much more or less?

A. Subject A (name):

Breaths in one minute at rest

Breaths after 15 seconds of exercise .... × 4 =

Is the breathing deeper after jumping?

B. Subject B (name):

Breaths during one minute at rest

Breaths after 15 seconds of exercise .... × 4 =

Is the breathing deeper after jumping?

C. Subject C (name):

Breaths in one minute at rest

Breaths after 15 seconds of exercise .... × 4 =

Is the breathing deeper after jumping?

IVA REVISION AND PREPARATION

Students will need to complete the following steps to meet the grading criteria of this unit:

- Prepare descriptions of the functions and structure of ALL of the following: skeletal muscular system, cardiovascular system and the respiratory system.
- Prepare movement checklists for THREE contrasting sports activities incorporating the muscles, joints and movement patterns.
- Carry out TWO basic tests to demonstrate breathing mechanics and changes in oxygen and carbon dioxide and record outcomes and results.
- List the immediate responses of the body to different types of exercise.

ANSWERS AND GUIDELINES TO WORKSHEET 5 THE SKULL

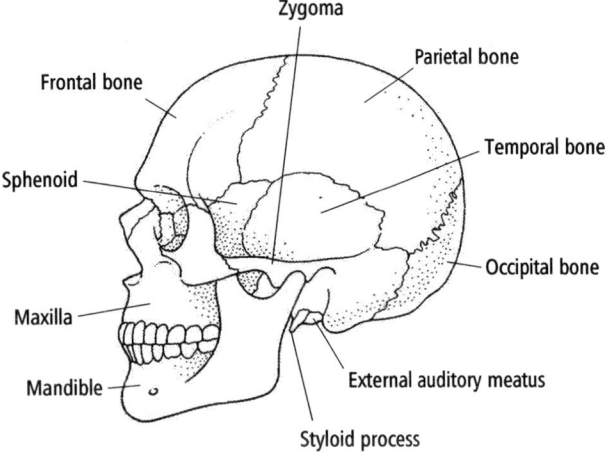

ANSWERS AND GUIDELINES TO WORKSHEET 6 THE SKELETON

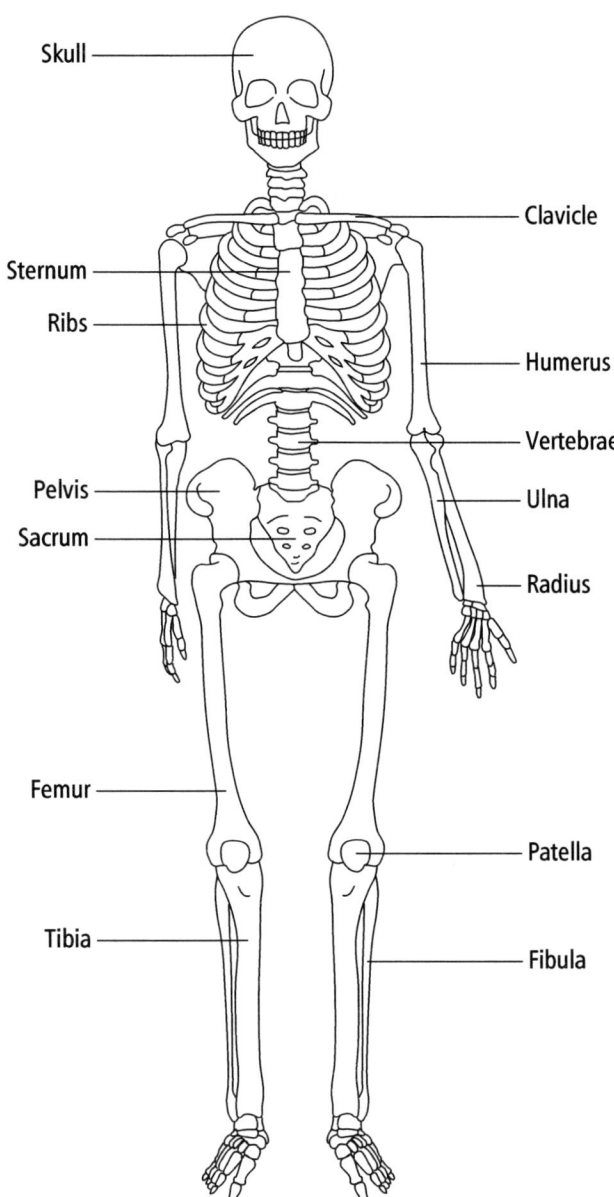

CHAPTER 4 – The body in sport

ANSWERS AND GUIDELINES TO WORKSHEET 7 THE SPINE

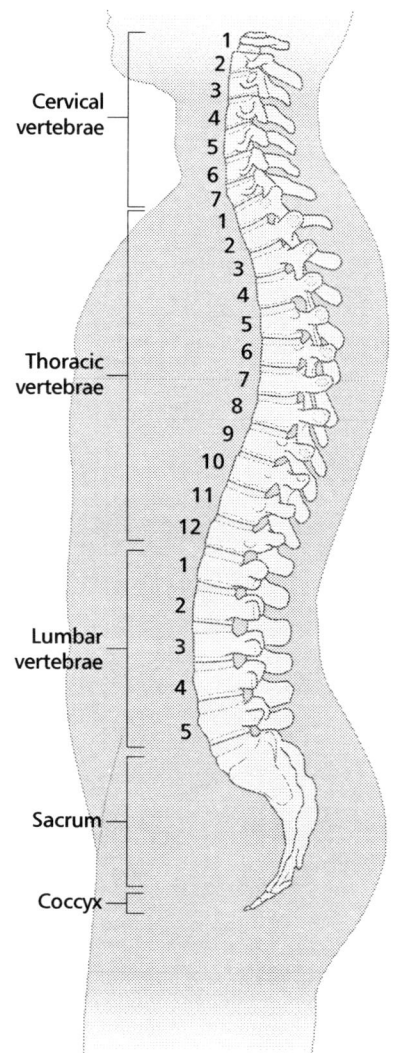

ANSWERS AND GUIDELINES TO WORKSHEET 8 THE HAND

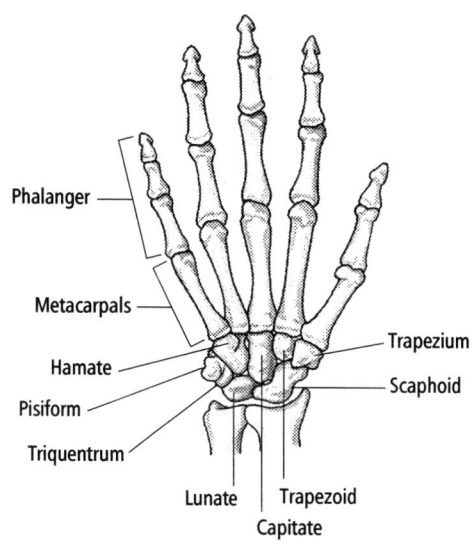

ANSWERS AND GUIDELINES TO WORKSHEET 9 THE KNEE JOINT

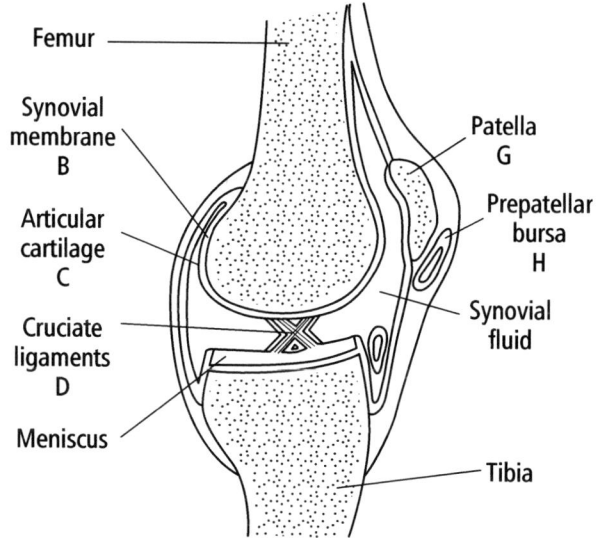

ANSWERS AND GUIDELINES TO WORKSHEET 10 CARTILAGE

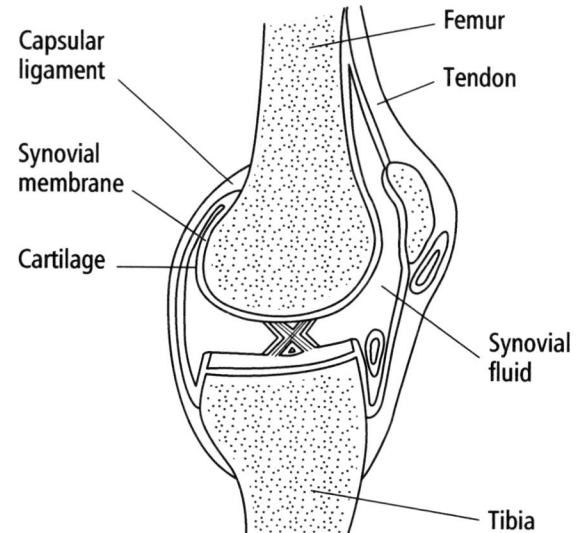

ANSWERS AND GUIDELINES TO WORKSHEET 11 TYPES OF MOVEMENT

The purpose of this exercise is for the students to think about the complex use of muscle groups that simultaneously operate to produce movement in the legs, upper body and other related parts of the body.

ANSWERS AND GUIDELINES TO WORKSHEET 12 MUSCLES OF THE BODY (ANTERIOR VIEW)

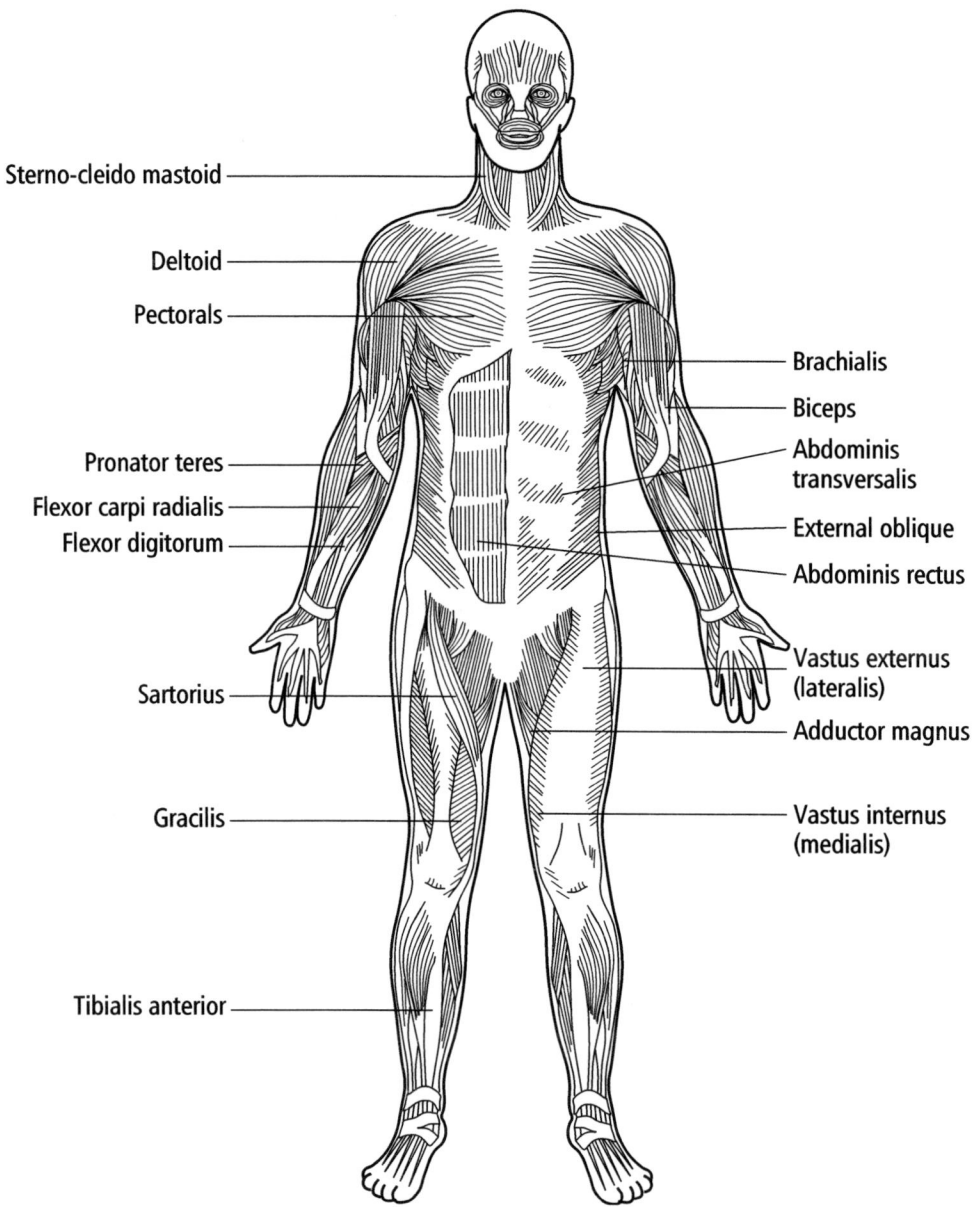

ANSWERS AND GUIDELINES TO WORKSHEET 13 MUSCLES OF THE BODY (POSTERIOR VIEW)

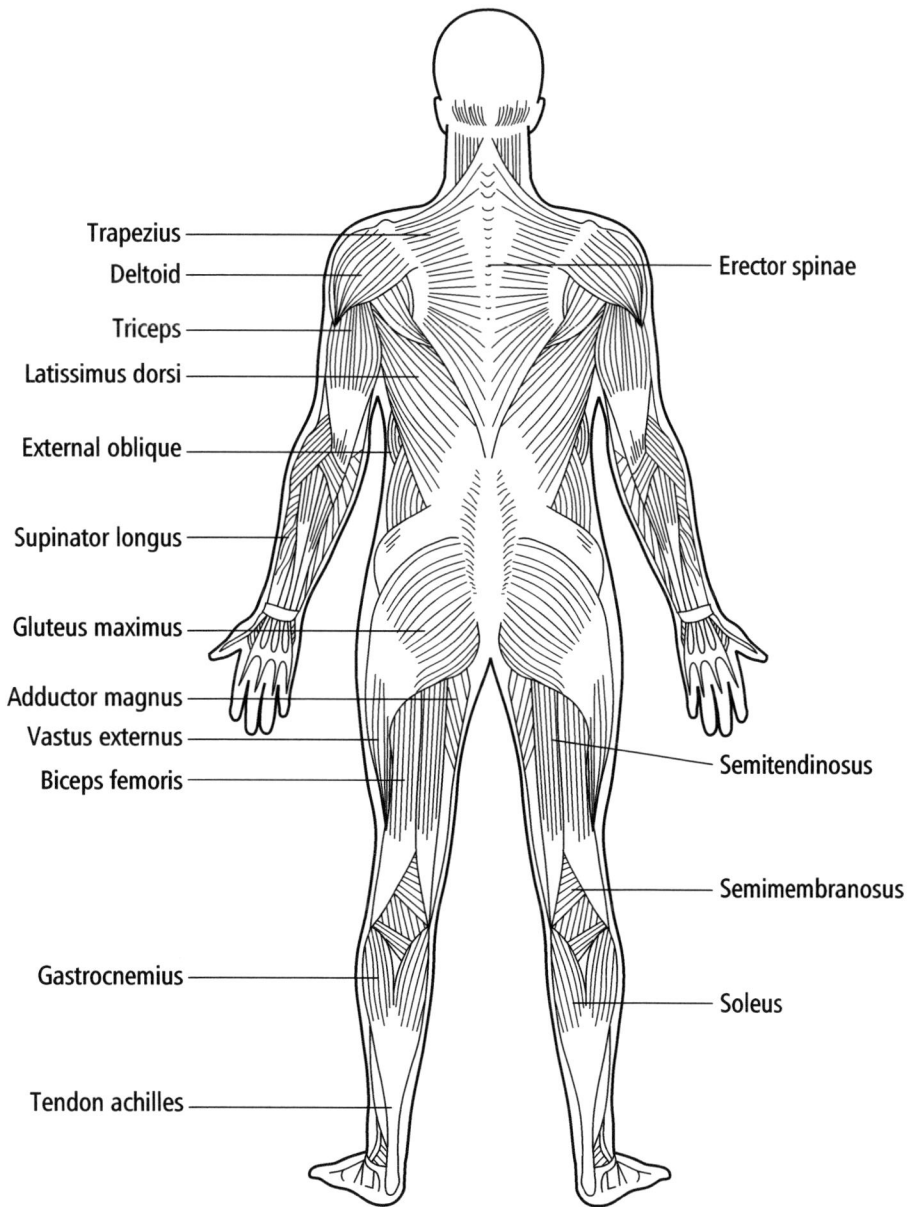

CHAPTER 4 – The body in sport

ANSWERS AND GUIDELINES TO WORKSHEET 14 MUSCLES OF THE EYE

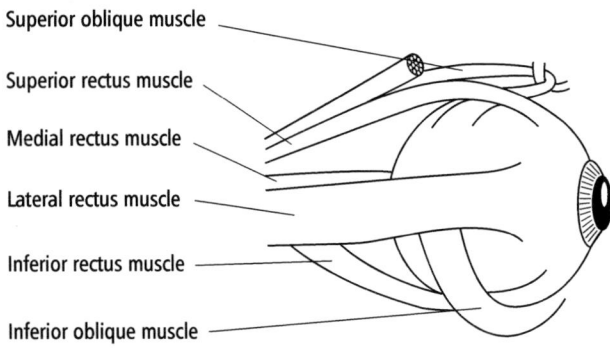

ANSWERS AND GUIDELINES TO WORKSHEET 15 FUNCTIONS OF MUSCLES

1. Sternocleidomastoid
2. Deltoid
3. Biceps brachii
4. External oblique
5. Sartorius
6. Tibialis anterior
7. Trapezius
8. Pectoralis major
9. Rectus abdominus
10. Rectus femoris.

ANSWERS AND GUIDELINES TO WORKSHEET 16 LEVERS AND ENERGY NEEDS FOR CONTRACTION

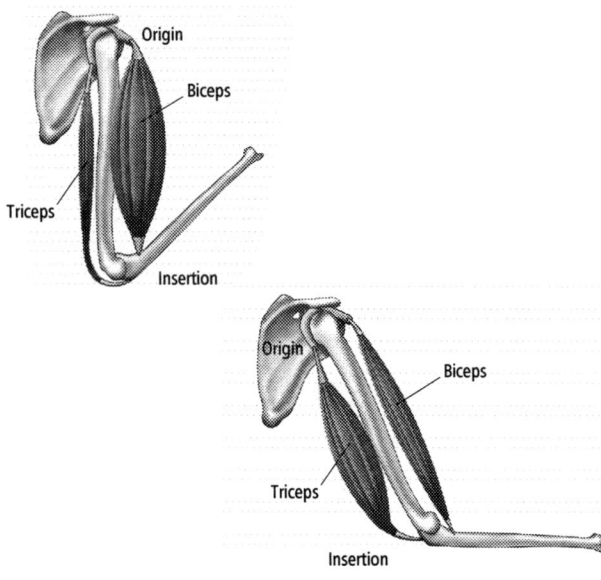

ANSWERS AND GUIDELINES TO WORKSHEET 17 STRUCTURE OF THE HEART

1. Deoxygenated blood from the body entering the heart.
2. The right atrium.
3. The valves prevent blood flowing the wrong way when the atria and ventricles contract.
4. The right ventricle.
5. The thicker-walled left ventricle.
6. The left atrium.
7. Oxygenated blood from the lungs entering the heart.
8. Oxygenated blood leaving the heart and flowing to the body.
9. Deoxygenated blood leaving the heart and flowing to the lungs.

ANSWERS AND GUIDELINES TO WORKSHEET 18 FUNCTION OF THE HEART

1. Right atrium
2. Tricuspid valve
3. Right ventricle
4. Pulmonary artery
5. Lungs
6. Pulmonary vein
7. Left atrium
8. Bicuspid valve
9. Left ventricle
10. Aorta.

ANSWERS AND GUIDELINES TO WORKSHEET 19 ARTERIES

1. Common carotid
2. Subclavian
3. Brachiocephalic
4. Ascending aorta
5. Brachial
6. Femoral
7. Talmar arches
8. Common iliac
9. Renal
10. Descending aorta.

ANSWERS AND GUIDELINES TO WORKSHEET 20 VEINS

1. Subclavian
2. Brachial
3. Basilic
4. Femoral
5. Posterior tibial
6. Great saphenous
7. Iliac
8. Inferior vena cava
9. Superior vena cava
10. Jugular.

ANSWERS AND GUIDELINES TO WORKSHEET 21 RESPIRATORY SYSTEM

1. Nasal cavity
2. Oral cavity
3. Larynx
4. Trachea
5. Lung
6. Bronchus
7. Alveoli.

ANSWERS AND GUIDELINES TO WORKSHEET 22 MECHANICS OF BREATHING

1. Cervical vertebrae
2. True rib
3. True rib
4. Floating rib
5. Lumbar vertebrae
6. False rib
7. Xiphoid process
8. Body of sternum
9. Manubrium.

ANSWERS AND GUIDELINES TO WORKSHEET 23 EFFECTS OF EXERCISE

1. The football player is breathing hard primarily because of excessive carbon dioxide and blood acidity. Although using the oxygen tank he is breathing in 100 per cent oxygen and his oxygen debt is being replenished very much more quickly, this does absolutely nothing for his CO_2 excess and blood acidity. The hiker truly has an oxygen depletion problem because there is less O_2 (and CO_2) at high altitudes. In contrast to the football player, the hiker does not have excess CO_2. Therefore oxygen from a tank can help his problem. (In fact the hiker may suffer from too little CO_2; as s/he ventilates more to help the oxygen problem, the hiker may blow off too much CO_2 and the blood could become basic (i.e. contain too little carbon dioxide). This 'alkalosis' is thought to cause most of the symptoms of mountain sickness.)

ANSWERS AND GUIDELINES TO CASE STUDY 4.1

1. For most of our waking hours, our blood pressure stays pretty much the same when sitting or standing still. The level should be lower than 120/80. When the level stays at 140/90 or higher, we have high blood pressure. With high blood pressure, the heart works harder, the arteries are stressed, and the chances of a stroke, heart attack and kidney problems are greater.

2. Lifestyle changes include the following:
   - Do not smoke cigarettes or use any tobacco product.
   - Lose weight if you are overweight.
   - Exercise regularly.
   - Eat a healthy diet that includes lots of fruits and vegetables and is low in fat.
   - Limit your intake of sodium, alcohol and caffeine.
   - Try relaxation techniques or biofeedback.

3. Hypertension is the medical name for high blood pressure. It is not a 'disease' in itself but it is a significant risk factor in other diseases including heart attack, stroke and kidney disease. In fact, the UK Government has estimated that over one-third of all deaths of people under 65 years of age are attributable to hypertensive causes.

ANSWERS AND GUIDELINES TO WORKSHEET 24 MUSCULAR SYSTEMS AND EXERCISE

1. Short-term effects on the skeletal system are minimal. However, in the long term the bones become stronger as the load-bearing nature of exercise encourages the process of ossification.

The muscular system responds to exercise by demanding more oxygen and nutrients, which are carried in the blood supply. If there is insufficient oxygen, lactic acid forms which fatigues the muscle. In the long term the blood supply to the muscles improves and muscular hypertrophy takes place (muscles become bigger) as a result of regular exercise.

Chapter 5: Sports leadership skills

The information on this page is intended to help you plan and deliver your lessons using BTEC First Sport *by John Honeybourne.*

OVERVIEW

This chapter introduces students to the skills, techniques and knowledge required to run sports, recreational and play activities. The purpose of the unit is to identify and use the skills and qualities needed. The precise purpose of the unit is to:

- Look at the skills and qualities required to lead a successful activity session and use them.
- Help in planning an activity session.
- Deliver and then review an activity session.

ADVICE AND GUIDANCE TO STUDENTS

Once the fundamental skills and qualities needed to run an activity session have been grasped, this chapter, overall, is a practical one. In order to appreciate what is required, the following table shows the key points:

PASS	To obtain a MERIT do this as well	To obtain a DISTINCTION do this as well
With teacher support, identify and use skills and personal qualities to lead two contrasting activities.	Do this independently.	Modify and adjust what you do to suit the needs of the participants.
With teacher support, produce a session lesson plan incorporating progression, timing, sequencing, health and safety needs and legal requirements.	Do this independently.	Critically analyse the plan and justify choices made. Provide examples of alternatives or modifications.
With teacher support, produce a contingency plan covering two situations offering alternatives.	Do this independently.	Critically evaluate and review your plan. Provide realistic modifications and alternatives.
Deliver and review the session. Comment on own role and identify skills acquired by participants and any changes to the activity.	Explain and justify changes.	Critically analyse the session and draw conclusions for your own development and that of the participants.

SUGGESTED LESSON PLAN

TOPIC	HOURS	ACTIVITY TO USE	PAGE
Skills and qualities Personal skills	7	Case Study 5.1 Exercise time management	124
		Worksheet 25 Communications quiz	125
		Worksheet 26 Communications quiz – additional exercise	126
		Worksheet 27 Health and safety quiz	127
Personal qualities	7	Worksheet 28 Leadership quiz	128
		Worksheet 29 Motivation quiz	129
		Worksheet 30 Are you in control?	130
Activities to choose	3		
Planning Lesson planning	7	Worksheet 31 Planning	132
Health and safety	3	Worksheet 32 Health and safety	133
Legal responsibilities	2	Worksheet 33 Legal responsibilities	134
Target groups	2	Case Study 5.2 Target groups for Brent	135
Contingencies	2	Worksheet 34 Contingencies	136
Action planning	3	Worksheet 35 Action planning	137
Deliver and review			
Organisational skills	4	Worksheet 36 Organisational skills	138
Activity session	6	Worksheet 37 Activity session	139
Review	4	Worksheet 38 Review	140
Modify	3	Worksheet 39 Modify	141
IVA revision and preparation	7		142

ANSWERS TO PROGRESS CHECK (PAGE 131, BTEC FIRST SPORT)

1 List four points that will make a sports leader's communication more effective.

Answer
Communication skills should include the following:

- directness
- consistency
- separation of fact from opinion
- avoiding overload by focusing on one issue at a time
- repetition of key points
- awareness of audience.

2 Make a list of things you need to organise before teaching a sports activity.

Answer
In order to be well organised you should:

- plan well in advance
- prepare and organise the facilities to be used
- carry out safety checks and prepare equipment
- work with others to develop a sense of team work
- plan the session to take into account facilities and ability of participants
- have a contingency plan ready in case the original plan does not go well or circumstances change.

3 What health and safety aspects should be taken into consideration before leading a sports activity?

Answer
Health and safety aspects should include:

- checking all of the equipment before, during and after the session
- checking that the facilities are safe
- ensuring that participants are fit enough to carry out the activity
- monitoring the safety of the participants during the session
- ensuring there is access to first aid
- awareness of emergency procedures.

CHAPTER 5 – Sports leadership skills

4   What factors affect the type of leadership style you choose?

Answer

The leadership style adopted is affected by:

- the situation
- the members of the group
- the personality of the leader.

5   What is meant by the whole-part-whole method of practice sessions?

Answer

The whole-part-whole coaching technique is the coaching of a complete skill, then teaching it in parts and teaching it as a whole again for a second time.

6   How can a demonstration be fully effective?

Answer

A demonstration needs to command the attention of the participant, providing them with prompts to ensure their focus. It also needs to ensure that the participants retain the information, and this is usually achieved as a result of clear demonstrations.

7   Construct a lesson plan for a sports activity of your choice for a group of 11-year-old beginners.

Answer

The student should take into account the textbook's recommendations, on p125, which looks at the characteristics of a good session. It should also take into account the health and safety aspects on pp126–7.

8   What makes a session poor?

Answer

There are several reasons why a session could be considered to be of low quality, including:

- the leader talking too much
- lack of activity by the participants
- lack of session purpose
- activity too difficult for the participants
- leader's inability to project their voice
- leader providing too much information
- leader allowing ill discipline
- carrying out the session in poor facilities or with poor equipment.

9   What is meant by a SWOT analysis?

Answer

S – Strengths – what went well in the session, what good things came out of it such as positive attitudes and skills learning.

W – Weaknesses – what did not go so well. Was there any misbehaviour or lack of concentration by the participants? Was there confusion over what was to be done and were the facilities poor etc.?

O – Opportunities – what could be done next time to improve, will you make the activities more fun or more demanding? Could you get into a full game sooner? Are the participants ready for some more advanced coaching related to tactics?

T – Threats – what barriers are there to these opportunities? There may not be enough equipment to go round. You may not have the advanced knowledge necessary for more sophisticated practices. There may not be enough time to achieve what you set out to achieve.

10   Evaluate any sports activity session that you have experienced or taken yourself. How would you make it better?

Answer

Obviously this answer will be an individual task carried out by the student. They should be advised to construct a simple SWOT analysis diagram and complete it to the best of their abilities.

CHAPTER 5 – Sports leadership skills

SKILLS AND QUALITIES

CASE STUDY 5.1
EXERCISE TIME MANAGEMENT

Even those who are not regularly involved in sports need a balanced programme of moderate physical activity. People are urged to spend 30 minutes a day exercising. This is beneficial even for people with chronic conditions of bones and joints. The 30 minutes can be broken into shorter periods such as 15 minutes gardening in the morning and 15 minutes walking briskly in the afternoon.

Here is a sample activity log that you can use to keep track of the minutes you spend on physical activity.

Activity	Mon.	Tues.	Wed.	Thurs.	Fri.	Sat.	Sun.
Brisk walking							
Gardening							
Mowing lawn							
Stretching exercises							
Weight lifting							
Jogging/running							
Aerobics							
Bicycling							
Stair climbing							
Swimming							
Tennis							
Bowling							
Golf							
Other sports							
Dancing							
Other activities							

QUESTIONS AND TASKS

1   Design your own version of the activity log to suit your activities.

WORKSHEET 25 SKILLS AND QUALITIES: COMMUNICATIONS QUIZ

Read these statements and rate each one with the number that best describes you. There are no right or wrong answers.

0 Never   1 Seldom   2 Sometimes   3 Often

1 I absorb information quickly. ....
2 I am talkative early in the morning. ....
3 I am talkative late at night. ....
4 I pay attention to visual details. ....
5 I give short, concise answers to most questions. ....
6 I keep most of my thoughts to myself. ....
7 Much of the time I am absorbed in my own ideas. ....
8 It is easy for me to identify my feelings. ....
9 I believe most of my thoughts are of interest to others. ....
10 I believe most of my thoughts are not of interest to others. ....
11 I believe most of my thoughts are not anyone else's concern. ....
12 I have difficulty expressing my thoughts. ....
13 I have difficulty expressing my feelings. ....
14 I base my decisions more on logic than emotions. ....
15 I like to talk about intimate and/or emotional matters. ....
16 I have a hard time knowing what I am feeling. ....
17 I feel overwhelmed or confused when people jump from one idea to another. ....
18 I am a fast talker. ....
19 I quickly tire of a subject. ....
20 I speak slowly, often pausing to think. ....
21 I feel bored or anxious if my partner talks too slowly. ....
22 I feel bored or anxious if my partner talks too quickly. ....
23 I like to be the centre of attention. ....
24 I vigorously defend my thoughts and opinions. ....
25 I like to talk about what I am feeling. ....
26 I like to have good conversations when I eat. ....
27 I do not like to talk when I eat. ....
28 I like to talk to someone when I am doing sport. ....
29 I do not like to talk when I am doing sport. ....
30 I do not like to talk about money or financial matters. ....

CHAPTER 5 – Sports leadership skills

WORKSHEET 26 SKILLS AND QUALITIES: COMMUNICATIONS QUIZ – ADDITIONAL EXERCISE

Now complete the following statements in a few words.

As a general rule, the times of day and general situation when I feel most available to talk are ....
....
....

I listen most attentively when people ....
....
....
....
(e.g. talk slowly, talk quickly, do not dwell on one subject too long, speak with enthusiasm, speak in a calm voice, share their emotions, etc.)

It is difficult for me to pay attention when people ....
....
....
....
(e.g. talk at length about work, jump from topic to topic, talk only about problems, etc.)

It is difficult for me to talk when ....
....
....
(e.g. people ask too many questions, I am tired, I first wake up, etc.)

WORKSHEET 27 SKILLS AND QUALITIES: HEALTH AND SAFETY QUIZ

QUESTIONS AND TASKS

1 What do the following signs mean?

Answer ....

Answer ....

 Answer ....

 Answer ....

CHAPTER 5 – Sports leadership skills

WORKSHEET 28 SKILLS AND QUALITIES: LEADERSHIP QUIZ

Try this quiz to see how you rate as a leader.

1. How important is status to you?
   - (a) Very important; you like to feel like you are in the top echelon.
   - (b) Quite important. It is good to be in with the in-crowd.
   - (c) It is more about the quality of relationships than where you fall within those relationships.
   - (d) Not very important; you just want to get on.

2. In your childhood what was your 'rank'?
   - (a) The leader: feared by all.
   - (b) The funny one: adored by all.
   - (c) The thinking one: listened to by all.
   - (d) The geeky one: noticed by none.

3. In class, do you come up with new ideas and suggestions?
   - (a) All the time, you really let everyone know what you think.
   - (b) Quite often, but not at all if it would mean upsetting someone.
   - (c) Often, being careful of any personal and political issues.
   - (d) Rarely. What if it was the wrong thing?

4. A fellow student has been criticised for shoddy work. What do you do?
   - (a) Tell them why they should have known better.
   - (b) Buy them lunch to cheer them up.
   - (c) Offer to proofread their next effort.
   - (d) Avoid them. You have too much to do as it is.

5. You have just faced some negative feedback. How do you respond?
   - (a) Get angry and defensive.
   - (b) Listen carefully but come away feeling disappointed.
   - (c) Consider what you could change and how you could improve.
   - (d) Sigh and think, 'Yeah, that is me.'

6. Do you think it is important to understand other's feelings?
   - (a) No, not really, why should you bother?
   - (b) It is an excuse to have a laugh about other people's fears.
   - (c) Yes, it is important.
   - (d) It is important so you can understand what buttons to press when you want them to do something.

7. Faced with a problem to solve, what do you do?
   - (a) Come up with one solution and pronounce it correct.
   - (b) Generate a few possible solutions and ask others what they think.
   - (c) Brainstorm with a couple of nearby colleagues.
   - (d) Seek your teacher's advice.

8. Your teacher has asked you to do something that is beyond your abilities. What do you do?
   - (a) Take it on; you are up to anything.
   - (b) Give it your best shot, making a passing joke not to blame you if it all goes horribly wrong.
   - (c) Agree to do the task, but ask for further direction and assistance.
   - (d) Stress out, clam up and finally confess that you just do not think you can manage it.

9. Is delegation:
   - (a) a waste of time. No one else will be able to do it as well as you, so you might as well do it yourself.
   - (b) an easy way to share the workload.
   - (c) an effective way to create new learning opportunities for others.
   - (d) something you are always on the receiving end of.

10. Change to you means:
    - (a) Something to be controlled.
    - (b) An opportunity where anything could happen.
    - (c) A chance to make progress.
    - (d) Something to go along with.

CHAPTER 5 – Sports leadership skills

WORKSHEET 29   SKILLS AND QUALITIES: MOTIVATION QUIZ

QUESTIONS AND TASKS

Consider your answers in the context of your current course and sporting achievements. To determine your dominant needs and what motivates you, circle the number that corresponds to your level of agreement with each statement (1 to 5, with 5 indicating that you agree strongly).

1	I try very hard to improve on my past performance.	1 2 3 4 5
2	I enjoy competition and winning.	1 2 3 4 5
3	I often find myself talking to those around me about non-work matters.	1 2 3 4 5
4	I enjoy a difficult challenge.	1 2 3 4 5
5	I enjoy being in charge.	1 2 3 4 5
6	I want to be liked by others.	1 2 3 4 5
7	I want to know how I am progressing as I complete tasks.	1 2 3 4 5
8	I confront people who do things I disagree with.	1 2 3 4 5
9	I tend to build close relationships.	1 2 3 4 5
10	I enjoy setting and achieving realistic goals.	1 2 3 4 5
11	I enjoy influencing other people to get my way.	1 2 3 4 5
12	I enjoy belonging to groups and organisations.	1 2 3 4 5
13	I enjoy the satisfaction of completing a difficult task.	1 2 3 4 5
14	I often work to gain more control over the events around me.	1 2 3 4 5
15	I enjoy working with others more than working alone.	1 2 3 4 5

BTEC First Sport Tutor Support Pack © Jon Sutherland, Nelson Thornes Ltd, 2005

WORKSHEET 30 SKILLS AND QUALITIES: ARE YOU IN CONTROL?

QUESTIONS AND TASKS

Consider the following pairs of statements. Choose the one from each pair with which you agree. As they have been picked to represent two extreme, opposing positions, it may be that you do not support either statement completely, but it is important to choose the one you agree with the most.

1. (a) Many of the unhappy things in people's lives are partly due to bad luck.
   (b) People's misfortunes result from the mistakes they make.

2. (a) One of the major reasons why we have wars is because people do not take enough interest in politics.
   (b) There will always be wars, no matter how hard people try to prevent them.

3. (a) In the long run people get the respect they deserve in this world.
   (b) Unfortunately, an individual's worth often passes unrecognised no matter how hard he tries.

4. (a) The idea that teachers are unfair to students is nonsense.
   (b) Most students do not realise the extent to which their grades are influenced by accidental happenings.

5. (a) Without the right breaks one cannot be an effective leader.
   (b) Capable people who fail to become leaders have not taken advantage of their opportunities.

6. (a) No matter how hard you try some people just do not like you.
   (b) People who cannot get others to like them do not understand how to get along with other individuals.

7. (a) I have often found that what is going to happen will happen.
   (b) Trusting to fate has never turned out as well for me as making a decision to take a definite course of action.

8. (a) In the case of the well-prepared student there is rarely, if ever, such a thing as an unfair test.
   (b) Many times exam questions tend to be so unrelated to course work that studying is really useless.

9. (a) Becoming a success is a matter of hard work; luck has little or nothing to do with it.
   (b) Getting a good job depends mainly on being in the right place at the right time.

10. (a) The average citizen can have an influence on government decisions.
    (b) This world is run by the few people in power, and there is not much the little guy can do about it.

11. (a) When I make plans, I am almost certain that I can make them work.
    (b) It is not always wise to plan too far ahead because many things turn out to be a matter of good or bad fortune.

12. (a) In my case getting what I want has little or nothing to do with luck.
    (b) Many times we might just as well decide what to do by flipping a coin.

13. (a) Who gets to be the boss often depends on who was lucky enough to be in the right place first.
    (b) Getting people to do the right thing depends upon ability, luck has little or nothing to do with it.

14. (a) As far as world affairs are concerned, most of us are the victims of forces we can neither understand nor control.

CHAPTER 5 – Sports leadership skills

WORKSHEET 30 (CONTINUED) SKILLS AND QUALITIES: ARE YOU IN CONTROL?

    (b) By taking an active part in political and social affairs people can control world events.

15 (a) Most people do not realise the extent to which their lives are controlled by accidental happenings.
    (b) There really is no such thing as luck.

16 (a) It is hard to know whether or not a person really likes you.
    (b) How many friends you have depends upon how nice a person you are.

17 (a) In the long run the bad things that happen to us are balanced by the good ones.
    (b) Most misfortunes are the result of lack of ability, ignorance, laziness, or all three.

18 (a) With enough effort we can wipe out political corruption.
    (b) It is difficult for people to have much control over the things politicians do in office.

19 (a) Sometimes I cannot understand how teachers arrive at the grades they give.
    (b) There is a direct connection between how hard I study and the grades I get.

20 (a) Many times I feel that I have little influence over the things that happen to me.
    (b) It is impossible for me to believe that chance or luck plays an important role in my life.

21 (a) People are lonely because they do not try to be friendly.
    (b) There is not much use in trying too hard to please people; if they like you, they like you.

22 (a) What happens to me is my own doing.
    (b) Sometimes I feel that I do not have enough control over the direction my life is taking.

23 (a) Most of the time I cannot understand why politicians behave the way they do.
    (b) In the long run, the people are responsible for bad government on a national as well as on a local level.

CHAPTER 5 – Sports leadership skills

WORKSHEET 31 PLANNING: PLANNING

QUESTIONS AND TASKS

Here is a blank lesson/session plan. You can use this as the basis of your planning for the sports activity required for this unit.

INSTRUCTOR		DATE
COURSE TITLE		LESSON NUMBER
UNIT	SPECIFIC TOPIC	

INSTRUCTIONAL GOAL (outcome that students should be able to demonstrate upon completion of the entire unit)
PERFORMANCE OBJECTIVE (use an action verb in a description of a measurable outcome)
RATIONALE (brief justification – why you feel the students need to learn this topic)
LESSON CONTENT (what is to be taught)

INSTRUCTIONAL PROCEDURES
    a. Focusing event (something to get the students' attention)
    b. Teaching procedures (methods you will use)
    c. Formative check (progress checks throughout the lesson)
    d. Student participation (how you will get the students to participate)
    e. Closure (how you will end the lesson)

EVALUATION PROCEDURES (how you will measure outcomes to determine if the material has been learned)
MATERIALS AND AIDS (what you will need in order to teach this lesson)

BTEC First Sport Tutor Support Pack © Jon Sutherland, Nelson Thornes Ltd, 2005

CHAPTER 5 – Sports leadership skills

WORKSHEET 32 PLANNING: HEALTH AND SAFETY

QUESTIONS AND TASKS

Here is a list of typical items from a sports first-aid kit:

Contents: 20 assorted plasters, two conforming bandages 8 cm, two conforming bandages 10 cm, two crêpe bandages 7.5 cm, one crêpe bandage 10 cm, two triangular bandages, one instant cold pack, two sterile large dressings, one 'skin-tact' dressing pad 5 cm × 5 cm, three 'skin-tact' dressing pads 10 cm × 10 cm, three sterile medium dressings, one eyewash 150 ml, one resuscitation face shield, one polythene apron, one biohazard disposal bag, 12 safety pins, wallet of five 'steristrip' suture strips, 10 alcohol-free wipes, one roll of micropore tape 2.5 cm, one pair of tough-cut scissors, four pairs of latex gloves, one pain-relief cold spray, one set of guidance notes.

1   Where would you obtain such a kit, or how would you assemble the items needed?

   Answer ....

   ....

   ....

   ....

CHAPTER 5 – Sports leadership skills

WORKSHEET 33 PLANNING: LEGAL RESPONSIBILITIES

QUESTIONS AND TASKS

Concerns about the difficulty of identifying safety standards at Adventure Activities Centres resulted (in 1995) in the Government introducing compulsory inspection and licensing for activity centres providing adventure activities to young people (17 years old and under).

1. Visit the web site of the Adventure Activities Licensing Authority at www.aala.org/providers.php and find out the names and addresses of groups that have been inspected and licensed in your area.

   Answer ....
   ....
   ....
   ....

CHAPTER 5 – Sports leadership skills

PLANNING

CASE STUDY 5.2
TARGET GROUPS FOR BRENT

Bridge Park Community Leisure Centre in Stonebridge is opening up its sports hall to sports-mad girls and boys over the summer holidays. A programme of sports activities will be available at Bridge Park for young people during the school holidays to help them occupy their time, keep active and have fun.

Every Monday through to Thursday morning (2 August to 27 August), boys and girls from 8–12-years-old can take part in multi-sports sessions. A wide range of sports equipment will be available from football, 'kwik' cricket, unihoc, basketball, netball, table tennis and much more to help entertain and wear out all those budding Olympians.

On Fridays, youngsters aged 8–12 (10 am-12 noon) and 5–8 (2 pm–4 pm) can enjoy a fun session that includes a bouncy castle and games and races. Each multi-sports session or fun session costs £2.50 per person.

Budding young tennis players can receive concentrated coaching from our experienced and qualified tennis coach. Youngsters aged 5–8 and 8–12 years can learn how to play different strokes, return passes and work towards playing a game. The mini-tennis lessons take place indoors using softer balls, smaller courts and rackets. Two four-day mini-tennis courses are being held in the afternoons during the school holidays and cost either £12 for four days or £3.50 per session.

For those who aspire to different heights, basketball coaching will be given by Bridge Park's resident basketball coach/player. Youngsters aged 8–12 can learn how to dribble, lay up, defend, shoot correctly and then put it all into a game situation. Two four-day basketball courses are being held during the school holidays and cost either £12 for four days or £3.50 per session.

QUESTIONS AND TASKS

Look at the range of sports activities offered by this London borough.

1. What kind of sports activities are targeted at different age groups in your area?

    Answer ....

    ....

    ....

    ....

2. Has this given you any ideas of what might suit children or younger sports enthusiasts?

    Answer ....

    ....

    ....

    ....

PLANNING

WORKSHEET 34   PLANNING: CONTINGENCIES

QUESTIONS AND TASKS

Visit the following web sites and find out about the indoor and outdoor facilities that allow people to participate in activities despite the weather:

- www.wycombe.gov.uk/leisure
- www.durham.gov.uk/durhamcc/usp.nsf/pws/tourism+-+tourism+Activities
- www.centerparcs.co.uk/b2b/sf_teamactiv.jsp.

Answer ....

CHAPTER 5 – Sports leadership skills

WORKSHEET 35 PLANNING: ACTION PLANNING

ACTION PLAN			
What needs doing?	Who will be responsible?	What resources will be needed?	When will it be carried out?

QUESTIONS AND TASKS

This is a simple action plan. It should provide you with the framework to consider the various requirements or steps to ensure that all resources and other preparation is in place for your sports activity.

CHAPTER 5 – Sports leadership skills

WORKSHEET 36 DELIVER AND REVIEW: ORGANISATIONAL SKILLS

QUESTIONS AND TASKS

If the sports activity is designed for children, it may be necessary to ensure that the parents or guardians of the children complete a parental permission/consent form. The following example shows you the necessary format of the form.

Standard Parental/Guardian's Consent Form

Anything written on this form will be held in confidence. Our coaches need to know these details in order to meet the specific needs of your child.

I give permission for my child to attend for training and playing sessions.

CHILD'S FULL NAME: ....

ADDRESS: ....

HOME TEL: .... AGE: ....
DATE OF BIRTH: .... MALE/FEMALE (Please circle)
NAME OF FRIEND ATTENDING: ....
EMERGENCY TEL (1): .... (2): ....
IF UNAVAILABLE CONTACT: ....
TEL: .... RELATIONSHIP TO CHILD: ....
NAME AND TEL OF G.P.: ....
CHILD'S MEDICAL NUMBER: ....
DETAILS OF ANY KNOWN ALLERGIES, CONDITIONS, MEDICATIONS BEING TAKEN:
....

ANY OTHER SPECIAL NEEDS, REQUIREMENTS OR DIRECTIONS THAT WOULD BE HELPFUL FOR THE COACHES TO KNOW: ....

I will inform the coaches of any important changes to my child's health, medication or needs and also of any changes to our address or the phone numbers given.

In the event of illness, having parental responsibility for the above-named child, I give permission for medical treatment to be administered where considered necessary by a nominated first aider, or by suitably qualified medical practitioners. If I cannot be contacted and my child should require emergency hospital treatment, I authorise a qualified medical practitioner to provide emergency treatment or medication.

I have been made aware that the organisation has developed a child protection policy and they are committed to ensuring the safety of my child by having:

- A coaches/volunteer charter
- Clear recruitment policy which includes vetting all coaches and volunteers
- A transport policy
- A photography policy
- An anti-bullying policy
- Disciplinary procedures
- A designated person for child protection
- Guidelines on confidentiality.

The organisation is committed to ensuring that any information gathered in relation to our youth academies meets the specific responsibilities as set out in the Data Protection Act 1998. The [NAME OF SPORT] development officer will store the above information on the youth academy database for a maximum of 12 months before re-registering the player if still associated with the club.

I confirm that all details are correct to the best of my knowledge and I am able to give parental consent for my child to participate in and travel to all activities.

Signature .... Parent/Guardian
Print Name ....
Date ....

Please return this form to the relevant Coach or Manager of your age group.

---

138 BTEC First Sport Tutor Support Pack © Jon Sutherland, Nelson Thornes Ltd, 2005

CHAPTER 5 – Sports leadership skills

WORKSHEET 37 DELIVER AND REVIEW: ACTIVITY SESSION

QUESTIONS AND TASKS

A warm-up should consist of:

- a gentle jog to circulate blood and oxygen to the muscles so that they have more energy to work with
- stretching to increase the range of motion at the joints
- sport-specific exercises and drills.

The warm-up should last between 15 and 30 minutes. Do not warm up too early. The benefits are lost after about 30 minutes of inactivity.

Match the following words with the blanks in the text below:

- exercise
- flexibility
- heart
- muscle
- oxygen
- temperature.

WARMING UP is often overlooked but should be part of your injury prevention routine. A good warm-up will:

- Increase the .... of muscles.
- Increase blood flow and .... to muscles.
- Increase the speed of nerve impulses – making you faster.
- Increase range of motion at joints (...............................) reducing the risk of tearing muscles and ligaments.
- A warm-up will not only help avoid injury but will also improve performance.

COOL DOWN: This is also often overlooked but can help to avoid injuries and boost performance. The aim of the cool-down is to:

- Gradually lower .... rate and breathing rate.
- Circulate blood and oxygen to muscles, restoring them to the condition they were in before ....
- Remove waste products such as lactic acid.
- Reduce the risk of .... soreness.
- The cool-down should consist of a gentle jog followed by light stretching.

CHAPTER 5 – Sports leadership skills

WORKSHEET 38 DELIVER AND REVIEW: REVIEW

QUESTIONS AND TASKS

In order to fully review the sports activity and to provide you with notes for comment for the IVA, it may be useful to ask another student to observe the activity using a form similar to the one outlined below.

To be completed by the observer

Preparation
e.g. Are the purposes appropriate and achievable? Were they communicated to the participants? Was the session related to participants' prior knowledge? Was the structure and progression of the session coherent? Were any constraints imposed by accommodation etc. taken into account?

Methods and Presentation
e.g. Was the choice of learning and teaching methods appropriate to the outcomes? Was the structure clear and the pace of the session appropriate?

Participation
e.g. What level of participation was expected? Was this achieved? Was active participant learning encouraged in the session? What was the atmosphere? Was awareness of individual participants' needs demonstrated?

What were the strengths of the session?

What areas could be the focus for further development?

What have you learnt from observing this session?

WORKSHEET 39 DELIVER AND REVIEW: MODIFY

QUESTIONS AND TASKS

Having reviewed your activity, you should now consider how you could have improved the session. You should also think about the following:

- What did the participants get out of the session?

  ....
  ....
  ....
  ....
  ....

- What did the participants learn that will be useful to them in the longer term?

  ....
  ....
  ....
  ....
  ....

- If you were to run the session again, what changes would you make?

  ....
  ....
  ....
  ....
  ....

IVA REVISION AND PREPARATION

In order to meet the grading criteria of this unit students should:

- List the skills and personal qualities required to lead TWO different sporting activities.
- Produce a lesson plan incorporating: the target group, progression, timing, the proposed outcomes of the session, and health and safety and legal requirements.
- Produce an action plan to deal with TWO contingencies (alternative activities, resources etc.).
- Deliver the session.
- Comment on and review the session from a personal perspective.
- Identify participants' skills acquisition.
- Suggest changes or modifications to the session in the light of experience.

ANSWERS AND GUIDELINES TO CASE STUDY 5.1

This activity should provide the basis for discussions and identification of the use of time, particularly in the context of sporting activities.

ANSWERS AND GUIDELINES TO WORKSHEET 25 COMMUNICATIONS QUIZ ADDITIONAL EXERCISE

Look for a pattern in the answers. The pattern exposes peoples' individual styles of conversation and communication. This personal insight will help when conversing with many different types of people.

ANSWERS AND GUIDELINES TO WORKSHEET 26 COMMUNICATION QUIZ ADDITIONAL EXERCISE

This is a follow-up exercise which should help students to recognise their key traits, specifically their listening and communication skills.

ANSWERS AND GUIDELINES TO WORKSHEET 27 HEALTH AND SAFETY QUIZ

The identification of these signs is a fairly straightforward task, but students could be asked to suggest where the signs may be found, either at a sports venue or training ground.

ANSWERS AND GUIDELINES TO WORKSHEET 28 LEADERSHIP QUIZ

How did they score?

Mostly As
You are a born leader just waiting for the right job to come along. You are strong, decisive and authoritarian. Everyone around you respects you. At least that is what you would like to think. In reality, the situation may be rather different.

Mostly Bs
You have good potential. You support people. You listen to others. You take the initiative. All this bodes well for your future, but only if you overcome what could become a fatal career flaw – wanting to be liked. There is nothing wrong with seeking out the approval of others.

Mostly Cs
Management, here you come. If you want to move up the ranks you probably have the ability to make that climb. You are creative, assertive and empathetic. You easily draw groups together and enjoy heading them up. Most promising though is the importance you give to developing the abilities of others. You have high expectations of them, possibly higher than they have of themselves.

Mostly Ds
You are smart enough to have figured out by now that your place is more likely to be in, rather than at the head of, the team. You prefer to listen to ideas, not voice them. You prefer to implement decisions rather than make them. This is not necessarily a bad thing.

ANSWERS AND GUIDELINES TO WORKSHEET 29 MOTIVATION QUIZ

High scores in the following questions indicate that achievement is the primary motivation:
1, 4, 7, 10, 13

High scores in the following questions indicate that power is the primary motivation:
2, 5, 8, 11, 14

High scores in the following questions indicate that affiliation (i.e. membership of a group) is the primary motivation: 3, 6, 9, 12, 15

Add up the total of each column. The column with the highest score indicates dominant needs and what motivates the student.

ANSWERS AND GUIDELINES TO WORKSHEET 30 ARE YOU IN CONTROL?

Score one point for each of the following answers:

1(a)	9(b)	17(a)
2(b)	10(b)	18(b)
3(b)	11(b)	19(a)
4(b)	12(b)	20(a)
5(a)	13(a)	21(b)
6(a)	14(a)	22(b)
7(a)	15(a)	23(a)
8(b)	16(a)	

Locus of Control refers to the extent to which individuals believe that they can control events that affect them.

The range of possible scores runs from zero (the lowest) to 23 (the highest), and your score will give you an idea of where you fall on the Locus of Control scale. There is no fixed dividing line between high, medium and low scores.

- High score: this means you have a high external Locus of Control. Those with a high external locus of control believe that powerful others, fate or chance primarily determine events.
- Mid-range score: most people are likely to fall roughly in the middle of the range. These people see themselves as being partly in control, but also significantly affected by outside events and circumstances.
- Low score: this means you have a high internal Locus of Control. Individuals with a high internal locus of control believe that events result primarily from their own behaviour and actions.

ANSWERS AND GUIDELINES TO WORKSHEET 31 PLANNING

This blank session plan should form the basis of the student's planning for their sports activity.

ANSWERS AND GUIDELINES TO WORKSHEET 32 HEALTH AND SAFETY

Several suppliers offer complete first-aid kits, for example:
- www.westonshealth.co.uk/acatalog
- www.firstaid-direct.co.uk

ANSWERS AND GUIDELINES TO WORKSHEET 33 LEGAL RESPONSIBILITIES

1. This area of the site allows the student to search for activity providers who are registered with the Licensing Authority as licence holders. Students need to select the area of Britain that they are interested in and a list of activity providers will be displayed on screen.

ANSWERS AND GUIDELINES TO CASE STUDY 5.2

1. A similar range of activities may be available in the local area.
2. This should give the students ideas about the types of suitable sports activities and alert them to the fact that the activity needs to cater for the target groups and may not correspond with the activity that the student is interested in providing.

ANSWERS AND GUIDELINES TO WORKSHEET 34 CONTINGENCIES

This search is designed to alert the students to the fact that their plans may be ruined if they do not have a contingency plan which allows them to carry out the activity at an alternative location.

ANSWERS AND GUIDELINES TO WORKSHEET 35 ACTION PLANNING

The action plan provided should be sufficient for students to note all of the resources and other items that need to be in place for their sports activity. The basic action plan covers the essential items of what, who, how and when.

ANSWERS AND GUIDELINES TO WORKSHEET 36 ORGANISATIONAL SKILLS

Parental permission is essential before undertaking a sports activity involving children. Equally, it must be made clear that permission is also necessary if the students are intending to photograph or video the event for evidence and later review.

ANSWERS AND GUIDELINES TO WORKSHEET 37 ACTIVITY SESSION

This is a simple activity designed to remind the students that the activity needs to be preceded by a warm-up and followed by a cooling-down session.

ANSWERS AND GUIDELINES TO WORKSHEET 38 REVIEW

It may be useful to pair up the students so that they can shadow one another during their sport activity session. The observing student should not be involved in the activity and will simply comment on the overall running of the event.

ANSWERS AND GUIDELINES TO WORKSHEET 39 MODIFY

When reviewing a training session, students could be encouraged to answer questions such as:
- What happened?
- What did I do?
- How did I do it?
- Why did I do it?
- How did I feel? Why?
- What did I learn?
- What does it mean?
- What should I have done differently?
- What do I need to do next time?
- What specific areas do I need to improve or extend?
- Which aspects were successful?
- What do I want to investigate further?
- How does this relate to previous knowledge and experience and to future learning activities?

CHAPTER 6

The sports performer

The information on this page is intended to help you plan and deliver your lessons using BTEC First Sport *by John Honeybourne.*

OVERVIEW

This chapter looks at the various factors that contribute to successful sports performance. The chapter covers skills specific to the sport in question and tactics related to that sport. It also considers fitness, diet, psychological factors, travel, competitive events, medical issues and financial support.

Specifically, the unit addresses the following issues:

- The factors that affect sports performance.
- Investigating opportunities to train and compete in two selected sports.
- The production of an action plan to improve performance in a sport.
- A review and evaluation of possible progress.

ADVICE AND GUIDANCE TO STUDENTS

This chapter is a practical one that seeks to assist students in either training or competing in a sport in the future. It asks them to review the factors that affect performances, to identify training and competition opportunities, to identify their own targets, record their progress and complete progress reviews. In order to understand the full implications of this unit the following table describes the requirements.

PASS	To obtain a MERIT do this as well	To obtain a DISTINCTION do this as well
List factors that affect sports performance in two different sports.	Describe these factors.	Compare the factors in the two sports.
Identify training and competition opportunities in three sports on a local, national and international basis.	Explain these opportunities.	Critically analyse these opportunities and suggest future developments.
With teacher support, identify SMART performance goals and targets and identify strengths and weaknesses.	Explain the SMART goals. Produce an action plan independently, which sets out targets, goals and training. Explain strengths and weaknesses to improve performance.	Produce and review an action plan independently, and justify the choice of targets, goals and training. Provide realistic alternatives.
Record your progress in a training diary over the period of one month.	Explain achievements.	Evaluate achievements and highlight areas for future development.
Using teacher support, regularly carry out progress reviews and identify areas for future development.	Do this independently.	Critically evaluate progress. Justify areas for future and further developments.

CHAPTER 6 – The sports performer

SUGGESTED LESSON PLAN

TOPIC	HOURS	ACTIVITY TO USE	PAGE
Factors that affect sports performance	7	Case Study 6.1 Coping with jet lag	148
		Case Study 6.2 Weaver back in business	149
		Case Study 6.3 GB coach runs wheelchair basketball training course	150
Opportunities to train and compete Training opportunities	4	Worksheet 40 Training opportunities	151
Opportunities to compete	3	Case Study 6.4 The Bank of Scotland	152
Types of competition	2	Worksheet 41 Types of competition	153
Action plan to improve performance Action plans	6	Worksheet 4 Personal action plan	154
Implementation	8	Case Study 6.5 Keeping a log	155
Evidence of possible progress Review	8	Worksheet 43 Review	156
Evidence of progress	8	Worksheet 44 Evidence of progress	157
Ongoing recording and review	8		
IVA revision and preparation	6		158

ANSWERS TO PROGRESS CHECK (PAGE 158, BTEC FIRST SPORT)

1 Give an example of a skill in your sport and state how you would practice it.

Answer
Students should realise that skills are learned and that they are improved by watching others and by practicing. Participants can pick up skills by carrying out specific tasks and by understanding the quality of a particular action and how it fits into the overall performance of the sport.

2 Explain an attack tactic in a team sport.

Answer
Attack tactics are used in many team and individual sports. A full example of how a tennis player uses attack skills can be found on p136, which considers Tim Henman's attack skills, including pressurising the opponent and hitting volleys.

3 In your sport, what are the most important components of fitness and why?

Answer
Students should choose from the full list of the components of fitness, and individual choices will depend on the sport involved. The main components should include some or all of the following:

- strength
- muscular or aerobic endurance
- flexibility
- power
- speed
- body composition
- agility
- co-ordination
- balance.

4 What psychological factors should be taken into consideration when performing your sport?

Answer
Students could suggest various psychological factors. These should include the following:

- level of motivation
- level of arousal
- ability to cope under pressure
- ability to concentrate
- mastering fears
- dealing with failure
- remaining calm and in control.

5 In your sport what sort of food should you consume on the day of competition and why?

CHAPTER 6 – The sports performer

Answer

This question will depend on the sport, but a balanced diet, particularly on the day of the competition, should include:

- carbohydrates
- proteins
- fats
- vitamins
- minerals
- iron
- calcium
- water.

6   Give an example of sponsorship in three different sports.

Answer

The range of sponsorship types is broad, but students could suggest sponsorship that falls into one of the following categories:

- sponsorship of an individual athlete
- sponsorship of the team's or individual's equipment or sports clothing
- sponsorship of a team or club
- sponsorship of a specific event.

7   How do athletes cope in a hot climate?

Answer

Dehydration is a considerable problem for athletes in hot climates. The body attempts to stay at 37 °C. Athletes start drinking fluids early on the day of the competition and around two hours before the event they drink up to 600 ml of fluid. A quarter of an hour before the beginning of the event they drink another 500 ml. During the event they will try to drink between 100 ml and 150 ml every 15 minutes. After the event they will drink more fluids.

8   What do physiotherapists do?

Answer

A physiotherapist is a trained individual who evaluates an individual's physical difficulties and helps them improve their movement and bodily function. They use exercise and heat manipulation to assist and improve mobility, balance, posture and fatigue.

9   What factors should you take into account when you are making an action plan to improve performance?

Answer

There are several factors, the most important of which are:

- the assessment of current performance
- targets for future performance
- performance planning
- monitoring and evaluation of performance.

10   How do you obtain evidence on how well you are doing in your sport?

Answer

This is obviously an individual question. A coach is a primary source of information. Specific factors could include:

- experience level reached
- technical knowledge and skills
- underlying abilities
- level of fitness
- commitment, training attendance and effort
- access to and willingness to use equipment and facilities
- effectiveness of the coach
- dietary discipline
- knowledge of areas requiring improvement
- methods of performance assessment used.

CHAPTER 6 – The sports performer

FACTORS THAT AFFECT SPORTS PERFORMANCE

CASE STUDY 6.1
COPING WITH JET LAG

Our bodies adjust to a natural rhythm that promotes sleeping at night and being active and alert during daylight hours. When we travel across different time zones our normal rhythm is altered. The sleep disturbance and loss of ability to concentrate, as well as the irritability felt during that time, is called jet lag.

The earth is divided into 24 time zones, and the time changes by one hour for every 15° of longitude travelled east or west of the Greenwich meridian. Travelling from London to New York necessitates turning your watch back by five hours, while travelling to Japan entails turning your watch forward by nine hours (nine time zones). Hence, if you travelled to Tokyo by plane from London, you might arrive at bedtime but your body would feel as though it was lunchtime. It takes time (about one day per time zone crossed) to adjust to local time.

In order to cope with jet lag you should get a good deal of sleep before your journey. It is also important to rest as much as possible during your flight. Allow time for adjustment on arrival.

Some people advise changing their watches to destination time when they board the plane. While this helps many people, for those who are on regular medication, such as diabetics, watches should remain on home time until they are able to adjust their medication to local times on arrival at their destination or as suggested by their health adviser.

On arrival at your destination get active as soon as possible and adjust your meals and activities to local time as soon as you can. Exposure to light is also a good way of allowing your body to adjust naturally.

QUESTIONS AND TASKS

Read the case study on jet lag and then answer the following questions:

1. Which is easy to cope with in terms of jet lag, travelling east or west?

   Answer ....
   ....
   ....

2. List three things that could intensify jet lag.

   Answer ....
   ....
   ....

3. Why might sports performers suffer from jet lag more acutely than others?

   Answer ....
   ....
   ....

CHAPTER 6 – The sports performer

FACTORS THAT AFFECT SPORTS PERFORMANCE

CASE STUDY 6.2
WEAVER BACK IN BUSINESS

On 14 December 2004 16 months of agony and torment came to an end for Manchester City's Nick Weaver. The former England under-21 keeper successfully came through last night's 4–1 reserve team defeat against Blackburn at Christie Park, Morecambe.

A chilly, wet 90 minutes on the Lancashire coast were the ideal test for Weaver's right knee that had been rebuilt in America in January this year in a revolutionary cartilage transplant operation.

The 25-year-old with more than 170 first team appearances behind him – including a starring role in the epic Wembley play-off win against Gillingham in 1999 – is the only top-class soccer star in this country to return to action after the ground-breaking, career-saving surgery in Cleveland, Ohio. In all, Weaver has been on the operating table five times and his last first-team league outing was nearly two years ago at Birmingham.

'There was a time when I thought this day might never come, so it was a bit emotional when I ran out,' said Weaver after the game.

'I came through well, my knee is fine but I have to say the groin and thighs are a bit sore. I did a lot more kicking than I expected I would but, yes, I am just delighted to get through it. I have been back in training now for perhaps a bit longer than people thought, but I know I still have a long way to go. This was my first step. I need another six or seven more of these and it should sharpen me up and I should be somewhere near.'

QUESTIONS AND TASKS

1   Read the case study about Manchester City's Nicky Weaver. Then find out what caused the injury and whether, at any point, it appeared that his career was over.

   Answer ....
   ....
   ....
   ....
   ....

CHAPTER 6 – The sports performer

FACTORS THAT AFFECT SPORTS PERFORMANCE

CASE STUDY 6.3
GB COACH RUNS WHEELCHAIR BASKETBALL TRAINING COURSE

The head coach of the GB Junior Wheelchair Basketball Team, Haj Bhania, is running a series of training sessions for wheelchair basketball coaches at Royal Holloway Sports Centre.

Royal Holloway Biochemistry student Helene Raynsford, who swims for Great Britain and is a wheelchair user, organised the training in collaboration with Royal Holloway's sports development officer John Salberg and Charlie Harlow, sports and societies administrator in the Students' Union. Helene is a member of Royal Holloway's STARS scheme, which awards bursaries to athletes who compete at national level and above.

Twelve people have signed up for the four-day course in Wheelchair Basketball Coaching, which leads to a coaching qualification that can be used in 'running' basketball. The participants are a mixture of wheelchair basketball and able-bodied running game coaches, sports developers and Royal Holloway students, representing a range of clubs: Sussex Sonics, Hampshire Harriers, Rushmoor Mallards, and Amazon Women's club Bognor Regis. Three participants are wheelchair basketball league players.

Wheelchair basketball is gaining popularity in the UK, boosted by the success of the national teams. The GB Men's Squad were silver medal winners at the 2002 Gold Cup (Wheelchair Basketball World Championships) in Kitakyushu, Japan in September 2002.

QUESTIONS AND TASKS

Read the case study on the wheelchair basketball coaching course and then answer the following questions:

1. What do you understand by the term 'bursaries to athletes'?

    Answer ....
    ....
    ....

2. Where could you attend a course for wheelchair basketball coaching?

    Answer ....
    ....
    ....

3. How did the GB wheelchair basketball team perform in the Athens Olympics?

    Answer ....
    ....
    ....

CHAPTER 6 – The sports performer

WORKSHEET 40 OPPORTUNITIES TO TRAIN AND COMPETE: TRAINING OPPORTUNITIES

QUESTIONS AND TASKS

The Talented Athlete Scholarship Scheme, or TASS as it is better known, is a Government-funded programme that represents a unique partnership between sport and higher and further education. TASS scholarships are for 18- to 25-year-olds (extended upper age limit of 35 for a scholar with a disability) who are undertaking higher or further education. TASS bursaries are for 16- to 19-years-olds (extended upper age limit of 35 for a bursar with a disability) who are undertaking further education or have left education to pursue a career.

1. What sports are covered in the TASS scheme?

    Answer ....
    ....
    ....
    ....
    ....
    ....

2. What disability sports are covered by the scheme?

    Answer ....
    ....
    ....
    ....
    ....
    ....

CHAPTER 6 – The sports performer

OPPORTUNITIES TO TRAIN AND COMPETE

CASE STUDY 6.4
THE BANK OF SCOTLAND

The Bank of Scotland provide generous support for athletics in Scotland in the following areas:

- Bank of Scotland Talented Young Athletes programme: a scheme designed to keep talented youngsters in the sport and help to develop them into Scotland's stars of the future. Now into its fourth year, the scheme has been a huge success.
- Bank of Scotland U20/U17/U15/U13 championships: by supporting both the indoor and outdoor National Championships, the Bank of Scotland helps Scottish athletics to deliver exciting competition opportunities for hundreds of young Scottish athletes.
- Annual Awards: in sponsoring the Scottish athletics Annual Awards, the Bank of Scotland helps to recognise the achievements of Scotland's leading senior, junior and veteran athletes.
- Commonwealth Games: in sponsoring the Scottish Commonwealth Games team, Bank of Scotland helps athletes to prepare for and to participate in the biggest event in which they can compete under a Scottish flag.

You can visit their web site at www.bankofscotland.co.uk/.

QUESTIONS AND TASKS

1   What similar competitive opportunities are available in your local area for your chosen sport? Find out the levels of competition available.

    Answer ....
    ....
    ....
    ....
    ....

WORKSHEET 41 OPPORTUNITIES TO TRAIN AND COMPETE: TYPES OF COMPETITION

QUESTIONS AND TASKS

1. Identify the opportunities to compete in at least THREE sports including your preferred sport in the region where you live.

   Answer ....

WORKSHEET 42 ACTION PLAN TO IMPROVE PERFORMANCE: PERSONAL ACTION PLAN

QUESTIONS AND TASKS

> **Be sure to make your action plan SMART:**
>
> - Specific: Be clear about your objectives/goals.
> - Measurable (or at least assessable): Will you know when you have achieved each goal?
> - Achievable: Are the goals achievable? Are they compatible with each other?
> - Realistic: Be realistic about the goals and the timescales.
> - Time specific: Be clear about when you want to achieve each goal, it is always possible to revise timescales if problems occur.

DESCRIPTION OF ACTION WITH TIMESCALE

e.g. I want to .... by ....

HOW WILL YOU ACHIEVE THIS? Identify smaller steps with timescales, people who can help, resources you need etc.

Goal 1

Goal 2

Goal 3

Goal 4

Goal 5

1 Complete a personal action plan to help you improve your performance.

CHAPTER 6 – The sports performer

ACTION PLAN TO IMPROVE PERFORMANCE

CASE STUDY 6.5
KEEPING A LOG

Much has been written about whether it is a good idea to keep a detailed training log and it seems that opinion will always remain divided. To an extent it depends on how serious the athlete is, although that is not always the case. For many enthusiasts it is the log itself that keeps them going and the daily entry becomes as much a part of the routine as the training itself.

QUESTIONS AND TASKS

1. What are the advantages and disadvantages of keeping a log? List as many pros and cons as possible.

   Answer ....

WORKSHEET 43 EVIDENCE OF POSSIBLE PROGRESS: REVIEW

QUESTIONS AND TASKS

Here is a sample log for a cardiovascular workout.

Goals and objectives

Warm-up

Cardiovascular workout				
Exercise	Programme	Level	Time	Progression

1 Design your own version to match the sport you are involved with.

CHAPTER 6 – The sports performer

WORKSHEET 44 EVIDENCE OF POSSIBLE PROGRESS: EVIDENCE OF PROGRESS

QUESTIONS AND TASKS

Throughout this chapter, you should be attempting to collect as much evidence as possible relating to your progress in your chosen sport. You should consider the following:

- results from competitions you have taken part in

  ....
  ....
  ....

- reports of your progress from teachers, coaches and tutors

  ....
  ....
  ....

- a series of fitness test results from the beginning of the unit to the end of the unit

  ....
  ....
  ....

- a series of dietary analysis reports

  ....
  ....
  ....

- analysis of videos of you engaged in sports activities

  ....
  ....
  ....

- analysis, from yourself and from observers, of you taking part in matches and events

  ....
  ....
  ....

- if possible, any press articles mentioning you by name.

  ....
  ....
  ....

CHAPTER 6 – The sports performer

IVA REVISION AND PREPARATION

Students will need to prepare the following to meet the grading criteria of this unit:

- A list of factors affecting sports performance using examples from TWO different sports.
- A list of opportunities to train locally, nationally and internationally for THREE different sports.
- An action plan including performance goals, strengths and weaknesses.
- A training diary over the course of a month.
- A series of progress reviews and an identification of areas for future and further development arising out of issues identified in the action plan.

ANSWERS AND GUIDELINES TO CASE STUDY 6.1

1. When you cross time zones, you arrive hours ahead of or behind the time in the country you flew from. The body has to adjust to new times of light, darkness and meals and often to a different climate.

   The problem is worse when travelling east because it is harder for the body to adapt to a slightly shorter day than to a slightly longer one. So, your body adapts better when travelling west because the day is extended, rather than travelling east, when the day is shortened. In other words, it is easier to delay sleep for a few hours than force yourself to sleep when you are not ready.

2. The effects of jet lag can be intensified by dehydration, tiredness, lack of sleep, lack of oxygen in the aeroplane cabin, alcohol and stress.

3. Those people who have a very strict routine tend to suffer most from jet lag. That is why children and babies, who can sleep almost any time, rarely show symptoms of jet lag.

ANSWERS AND GUIDELINES TO CASE STUDY 6.2

1. Weaver damaged his knee in a Division One match at Birmingham City in March 2002. In 2003, Kevin Keegan confirmed that Weaver faced surgery because of the recurrence of a long-term knee injury, leaving the Manchester City boss in a rush to complete either a permanent or loan signing once the January transfer window opened.

   'We have to wait to get Nicky to America (for expert medical attention) – but if I am honest we are probably going to have to forget about him for a year,' Keegan said at the time, 'He is definitely going to need some sort of operation. But we still think that when the operation takes place, which could be in the next three or four weeks, he has a great chance of coming back.'

ANSWERS AND GUIDELINES TO CASE STUDY 6.3

1. A bursary is usually a means-tested grant for athletes to allow them to concentrate on their sport.

2. There is now a level one and two Wheelchair Basketball Coaching qualification offered at some of the larger sports activity centres around the country.

3. A fantastic team performance saw GB win the Bronze Medal game 82–66 against the Netherlands. After finishing the first quarter four points behind, 18–22, GB dominated the three remaining quarters with outstanding team play.

ANSWERS AND GUIDELINES TO WORKSHEET 40 TRAINING OPPORTUNITIES

1. Archery, athletics, badminton, basketball, boxing, canoeing, cricket, cycling, diving, equestrian, golf, gymnastics, hockey, judo, modern pentathlon, netball, orienteering, rowing, rugby league, rugby union, sailing, shooting, skiing, speed skating, swimming, squash, table tennis, tae kwon do, tennis, triathlon, waterskiing, women's football.

2. Archery, athletics, swimming, equestrian, power lifting, boccia, judo, table tennis, wheelchair tennis, sailing, shooting, wheelchair basketball, fencing, cycling, wheelchair rugby.

Additional information can be found at www.culture.gov.uk/sport/tass.htm.

ANSWERS AND GUIDELINES TO CASE STUDY 6.4

1. Opportunities may be available at school/college or club, and at county, regional, national and international level. Note that competition will also be present at junior and senior levels.

ANSWERS AND GUIDELINES TO WORKSHEET 41 TYPES OF COMPETITION

1. Students should identify the opportunities to play in friendly games, leagues and various championships.

ANSWERS AND GUIDELINES TO WORKSHEET 42 PERSONAL ACTION PLAN

1. Students should identify up to five goals which they aim to accomplish during their time on the course (personal, academic, work related and so on). It is also useful to think about why they want to achieve each goal and how important the goals are to them. They may have to prioritise their time and focus on one or two areas. Students should identify how they might achieve these goals. Most goals can be broken down into smaller steps.

ANSWERS AND GUIDELINES TO CASE STUDY 6.5

1. The advantages of keeping a log are:
    (a) It acts as an update of your progress. You can include times, weather conditions and heart rate if you use a monitor, which can all help you learn and develop.
    (b) It acts as a motivator. By adding another entry you are one step nearer your goal.
    (c) It 'encourages' you to get out and do it. You know that you will feel bad in a few days time if you look back in the log and see a gap for no good reason.
    (d) It can serve as a reminder if you achieved a good performance and want to try and repeat it with the same training programme.
    (e) It can also serve as a reminder of training plans that did not work out and ones that should therefore be avoided in the future.

    The disadvantages of keeping a log are:
    (a) Some say that it makes the athlete compulsive and obsessed with the sport.
    (b) Others say that it makes athletes train when they should not, for example when they have an injury or when they are unwell, just so they do not miss an entry in the log.
    (c) Other critics say that comparing training plans from years before in a training log can be misleading, as conditions and personal circumstances could have been different.

ANSWERS AND GUIDELINES TO WORKSHEET 43 REVIEW

A typical training log could look like this (*see over*):

ANSWERS AND GUIDELINES TO WORKSHEET 44 EVIDENCE OF POSSIBLE PROGRESS

These pieces of evidence form the backbone of the IVA in terms of the student being able to show progression. Students should be informed that this is necessary from the outset of the unit, possibly before they even start the unit.

CHAPTER 6 – The sports performer

Goals and objectives
Weight loss, gains in fitness and stamina etc.

Additional information
Note: Your maximum heart rate is equal to 220 minus your age For example: A 30-year-old would have a max. heart rate of 220 – 30 = 190 beats per minute

WEEK 1

Workout days	3 alternate days
Workout time	20 minutes of continuous work
Equipment	Treadmill and bike
Intensity	70 per cent of heart rate maximum
Notes	Break down 20-minute workout time over the three machines suggested above

WEEK 2

Workout days	3 alternate days
Workout time	25 minutes of continuous work
Equipment	Treadmill, bike, rower
Intensity	70 per cent of heart rate maximum
Notes	As above

WEEK 3

Workout days	3 alternate days
Workout time	20 minutes of continuous work
Equipment	Stepper and treadmill
Intensity	75 per cent of heart rate maximum
Notes	As above

WEEK 4

Workout days	3 alternate days
Workout time	25 minutes of continuous work
Equipment	Treadmill, bike, rower
Intensity	75 per cent of heart rate maximum
Notes	As above

WEEK 5

Workout days	3 alternate days
Workout time	25 minutes of continuous work
Equipment	Stepper, rower, cross-trainer
Intensity	80 per cent of heart rate maximum
Notes	As above

WEEK 6

Workout days	3 alternate days
Workout time	40 minutes of continuous work
Equipment	Treadmill, bike, rower, cross-trainer
Intensity	70 per cent of heart rate maximum
Notes	Workout on each machine for 10 minutes, making a total of 40 minutes exercise time

CHAPTER 7: Work-based project

The information on this page is intended to help you plan and deliver your lessons using **BTEC First Sport** *by John Honeybourne.*

ANSWERS TO PROGRESS CHECK (PAGE 172, BTEC FIRST SPORT)

1 What makes a good curriculum vitae (CV)?

Answer

The key points are:
- Keep the CV simple, concise and straight to the point.
- Make the CV easy to read, avoid jargon and make sure there are no typing errors.
- Concentrate on the positive as it is a document designed to impress.
- Ensure any referees have been contacted before their details are included.
- Only include relevant information.

2 Why is a covering letter important?

Answer

A covering letter is important for the following reasons:
- It allows the candidate to explain aspects included in the CV.
- It gives the candidate the opportunity to highlight key aspects of the CV relevant to the post in question.
- If handwritten, it gives the employer the opportunity to assess the candidate's true literacy skills and neatness of handwriting.

3 Give five guidelines for someone who is going for an interview for a sports-related placement.

Answer

There are several points to consider, including the following:
- Do a trial run to make sure you arrive on time.
- Make sure you know who to ask for when you arrive.
- Dress appropriately.
- Have a thorough working knowledge of the organisation.
- Try to anticipate the type of questions that will be asked and formulate suitable answers.
- Ensure you take with you any relevant certificates or documentation to support what you have claimed in your CV.
- Make sure your CV is up to date.
- Be honest when replying to questions.
- Smile, be polite and positive.

4 Write down four things that you should not do at an interview.

Answers

There are several points to remember, including the following:
- Do not smoke.
- Do not swear.
- Do not yawn or show disinterest.
- Do not talk too much or too little.
- Do not be late.
- Do not be too familiar.
- Do not assume you are going to get the job.

5 Identify what preparation you need for an interview.

Answer

The list includes those points contained in the answer to question 3, but specifically, as outlined in the textbook, students should:
- know where and when the interview is
- work out an alternative means of getting to the location (for example, in case the bus does not turn up!)
- know who they have to meet and where.

6 Suggest a typical interview question and then write the answer that may help to secure the position.

Answer
Typical interview questions are detailed on pages 167–168 of the textbook, for example the questions regarding life at college, time in previous employment, future plans, why the individual wants the job or placement, and an identification of strengths and weaknesses. Other questions could include the interviewee's reading habits, their ability to deal with difficult situations, how they adapt to different people and situations, and general questions about the interviewee.

7 How would you record information effectively for your project?

Answer
The textbook recommends four types of recorded evidence. These are:
- placement logs or diaries of what has been learned
- personal accounts of observing others at work
- witness testimonies
- points requiring action relating to skills that need to be developed.

8 Identify how you would monitor and review your project

Answer
The textbook recommends that the student has a clear understanding of their aims, objectives and targets. It also suggests that the following are monitored:
- skills acquired on placement
- activities or coaching activities undertaken
- ways in which the monitoring has been carried out, including interviews, witness testimonies, videos and tape recordings.

9 Choose a career in sport and write down what qualifications and experience you need to get such a job.

Answer
Students should be cautioned to choose a realistic job for which they have a reasonable expectation of acquiring the necessary skills and qualifications. Typical long-term sports-related jobs could include the following:
- sports centre worker
- fitness instructor
- coach
- development officer
- sports scientist
- professional sportsperson
- grounds person
- sports therapist.

10 What makes a good project presentation?

Answer
The textbook recommends the following guidelines for the good presentation of a student's project:
- Use the past tense.
- Ensure that the writing is simple and clear.
- Write in sentences and check spelling.
- Ensure that mistakes or omissions are dealt with.
- Ensure paragraphs are not too long.
- Break up the project with headings.
- Number the pages.

In addition, students should include, in the form of appendices, any supporting evidence mentioned in the project. There should be a bibliography giving details of any information sources used and an introduction detailing the aims and objectives of the project. Statistical material should be presented in the form of graphs or tables. Students should cross-reference any audiovisual materials and include a copy of the presentation (using software such as *Microsoft PowerPoint*) which they have prepared along with the notes for that presentation. The conclusions should relate to the aims and objectives in the introduction.